FIRE IN MY HEART

fire in my heart

Nandini

ADVAITA SPIRIT
GLASTONBURY

Published by:
Advaita Spirit
36 Windmill Hill Road
Glastonbury
Somerset BA6 8EQ
UK

Email: ~~bishop@arunachala.fsworld.co.uk~~ nandinigrace@gmail.com

Internet: www.advaitaspirit.org

ISBN: 81-7525-586-2

Cover illustration: Mandala by Nandini Bishop;
photography by Roger Bishop & David Titchener

Cover & book design: Dev Gogoi

Printed at:
All India Press
Kennedy Nagar
Pondicherry—605001
India

contents

preface

'FIRE IN MY HEART' is indeed an apt title for this beautifully written book, appropriate because it tells a brave woman's story of a spiritual adventure in Consciousness, from childhood to an undoubted Awakening from the deep sleep of life. Nandini is a lady of integrity and authenticity. She was fortunate insofar as she was born into a spiritual family where her natural inclination for a search into the real meaning of life had fertile soil from which to grow. A few human beings are blessed with auspicious beginnings and it is very good that this should be so. Then we can all benefit from the close reading of an enthralling spiritual journey such as in this book.

As well as being a gifted writer and poetess she is a skilled artist. Her colourful and harmonious Mandalas best demonstrate the depth of her spirit, where the awakened inner Self is expressed in her paintings, which grace many a Glastonbury home. There has always been some quality very special to Glastonbury, the heart of Mystical Christianity in England, and Nandini and family have long been resident near the Tor. Although a Christian by upbringing, she developed a freethinker's approach in her search for truth. She explored the different traditions and with her supportive husband Godfrey went into the heart of Buddhism. But it was eventually to be the teachings of Ramana Maharshi and the Advaita Vedanta Philosophy which brought about a perspective change in Consciousness which we term Spiritual Awakening, the culmination of a long, ardent and earnest journey.

I heartily recommend this book to all those similarly engaged on the spiritual quest. They will discover many insightful jewels of wisdom in its delightful pages where poetry and prose are interposed. This book which it is a great joy to read will inspire many engaged in the most important step any human being can make, to know one's Self.

ALAN JACOBS

Chair, Ramana Maharshi Foundation, London, UK

foreword

IN OUR WORLD beyond 'these here' worlds, the sky is an ocean, is sky. Which is the viewer, which mirror, which is reflection - cannot be distinguished, for the Mind the painter, with mind the brush, mind the innumerable shades of the spectrum of hues, paints upon mind the wall, the mind the mural — so says *Yoga Vasishta*, the lyrical epic of the yogis. The lightning and the white crest on the waves are one and the same. It is all *akasha*, the sky and the space that is pure brilliance through which rays, strands, strings of brilliance pass to and fro, yet remain the epitome of stillness, in the hour that is night known as Dawn. Night, for it is still, it blankets, protects, shades, tucks the soul into repose; Dawn of enlightenment.

The soul is but a wave in this sky ocean of brilliance, a vibration finer than ten thousandth of a hair breadth, encompassing all of the ocean — yes, the wave of the ocean in which the ocean is a wave of its own wave. How can that be possible? In this trans-logical world. Oh, before I complete the sentence... 'this' commonly refers to what is here and now wherever we are and 'that' is something distant; for the one to whom the en-dawnment has been endowed what is 'beyond' for the many becomes 'this here' and the ones back in the village are then referred to as 'that', 'those'. Thus, in 'this' trans-logical world, a little of which peeks through the quantum physics where a photon is both a wave and a particle, the soul is the wave of the ocean that is a wave in the wave that is the ocean.

Some quiver at such a thought. Some cringe from it in fear and give themselves the titles of 'rational', 'atheist', 'agnostic', 'cynical', 'sceptical', 'non-believer'; logical.

A few have not forgotten their celestial home; their memories linger. A distant flute calls and calls. The heart become a drumbeat to the rhythm of the divine flute. On the time and space twin banks of the river of being's flow, He keeps playing his flute, plaintive, beckoning, commanding, invoking nostalgia, inviting come, come, come; hither; I am here, from your old Home in the Heavens; I call you, Oh soul, you that I am! Come, Oh I-You, come; Be with Me; Be Me: Be You the Self that is All. Come to the Home that is You-I.

Some, even at the moment of being swathed in the body to be wrapped in the placenta to be enwombed in the flesh-mother to be bound and gagged by chords of impressions of this-worldly passions, yes, even at the moment of being made a glob to be stuck to the linings of a flesh-mother's womb, have not forgotten; their soul-mind ears remain acute. They never cease to hear; never quite get bound and gagged. The glimpses flash; the sea-waves of the divine brilliance keep washing on the shores and beaches of their minds. The high tide may not remain at all hours, the moon waxes, then wanes, then waxes again. But it keeps bringing reminders, reminiscences, nostalgia. The brilliance may take the form of a being of light, a *siddha*, a disembodied Master, or may actually assume the form of a monk come begging at the doorsteps, come to claim what is his own. Or just a wave of light may wash over the body and the soul and for a moment — that is a mere moment to the 'this here' bound — an eternity passes through the soul. Just a reminder, I am still here, I was here when you writhed in confusion. I was here streaming through your window when you thought you were engulfed in darkness. I was here when you wooed the world and were offered earthly roses and smiles; I was that smile and you did not recognise Me. I am here now. I am that I am.

Nandini — the one (fem.) who enjoys and delights — has been such a soul. It is not by coincidence that soul waves meet soul waves and become siblings in a spiritual womb. The streams of the flowing notes of the Divine flute carry them gently, unknowing, towards each other. They meet in Gloucestershire and share what is worthy to be shared then; 42 years later they meet again, at the Ashram in Rishikesh.

Now, the thimble has become a large silver bowl into which much more can be poured. Some day the soul will make itself into the wine and offer itself in a golden chalice large as the ocean-sky of interior heart and the one who played the flute will now drink this soul and will make it One.

Nandini has expressed the imprints of the moments when eternity of brilliance passed through her soul. Some may read this writing as her narrative and poetry. No mere verbal poetry this, but a description in the exactitude. She has spoken of the unspeakable, ineffable, the undecipherable, the indescribable. Only in the language that to others appears to be poetic, she 'describes' how the light-notes of the Flute have enchanted her soul-ear throughout her this, the current body life.

May those who read, remember, reminisce, become nostalgic, long, long and long; may the book drop from their hands as they suddenly hear the Light and see the Sound; their longings answered, responded to, and then they just belong, and become a drop in the wine that the Lord will drink to celebrate their en-Dawnment.

Congratulations, Nandini, that you can so brilliantly depict the illumination the glimpses of which the Grace has shown you. What herein is beautiful is Hers; what herein might be of a stain on the lunar orb is yours that She will in time and beyond time wash away to make the fabric of your mind yet smoother, yet sweeter, yet more of the Dawn.

May 'you' cease to be so She may ever walk in You.

Swami Veda Bharati

Swami Rama's Ashram,
Rishikesh, India

introduction

*'May the thread of my song
be not cut before my life merges
in the sea of love.'*

(Source unknown)

THIS STORY BEGAN as a collection of 'inspirational' writings which came from Source. Something brilliant had happened and there was a need to write it down.

At the time of first writing, I was on a counselling course at our local college and we had all been invited to write our own life story. I found myself writing two books: my 'life story' for college and 'inspirational' writings just for myself. In the midst of all this, I went with my husband to South India for our first visit to Bhagavan Sri Ramana Maharshi's ashram in Tiruvannamalai, at the foot of the sacred mountain, Arunachala. I took these 'inspired' writings with me and had them blessed by the priests at the shrine of Sri Ramana Maharshi. I trusted that things would become clearer as to what to do with them all. Several friends had taken the time to read them and one of them suggested that they could be published. 'Great! but make it more personal,' seemed to be the unanimous suggestion. So, out of these 'outpourings' this story emerged and I began the process of rewriting up in our mountain retreat in Southern Spain some two years later.

NANDINI

Sierra de Niguëlas, Spain
July 2004

acknowledgements

MY THANKS and sincere gratitude go to Sri V.S. Ramanan for his enthusiasm and help, and to the priests at the Shrine of Sri Ramana Maharshi for blessing the script. To Sri Dev Gogoi for emanating as the artistic impulse behind the book's final shape and appearance and to Sri D. Vasudevan for his invaluable help. To Alan Jacobs, who has encouraged me every step of the way. To David Godman and Tony Parsons who gave good, professional advice. To Alexandra Rice, who was really enthusiastic and helpful in proof-reading. To the late Leonard Sleath for his valuable advice. To Karl Riley who was very interested and so encouraging. To Dr. Donald Jenkins who gave me the 'missing link' that was needed to complete the book. To my parents for giving me the opportunity to grow. To Nicolas, my elder son, who frequently encouraged me down the telephone line from Italy. My younger son, Charlie and daughter-in-law, Katharina were really inspired by the script and gave me their honest and heartfelt feedback. To my husband, Godfrey for his encouragement and help in proof-reading and editing the manuscript.

NANDINI

Glastonbury 2005

dedication

This work is humbly offered at the Blessed lotus feet of
Bhagavan Sri Ramana Maharshi
without whom the inspiration to write anything at all
could not have happened.

To all the spiritual teachers who have been important
signposts along the way.

To all who sincerely seek out the Truth and
wish for the Liberation of all beings.

arunachala speaks

On a cushion, immersed in deep silence, I sit in front of a photograph of

Bhagavan Sri Ramana Maharshi...

Stillness pervades the room.

Bhagavan's eyes are alive and smiling and I dissolve into an Ocean of Nectar.

At once, an almighty power descends,

Filling my heart with a love of indescribable joy and bliss.

Instantly, the great and holy hill Arunachala surrounds me.

Its vast stillness embracing me with life-giving energy,

Filling my whole body and mind with ephemeral light.

A supreme shaft of light and power runs through my body culminating in

A great blaze of light in the crown of my head.

This, the supreme embrace as 'I' dissolve into one living, pulsing light vortex.

The merging of the personal self with the all encompassing Infinite Self.

Like water mixing with water.

The embrace of two lovers:

The Lover and the Beloved;

The Guru and the disciple...

My heart is on fire...

my home

This life has been one long road to the Centre, my Centre.

My Home.

Many times did I stop to stare

To search the blue sky for a glimpse of Truth.

To share the dance of life with a tiny bird,

To admire a dew-kissed daisy...

My mind would step aside for a fleeting instant

And in that moment,

Eternity would step right in

And dance in the Light.

That Light, my very Being.

And I would KNOW

I am Home.

growing up

"...Tenderness
Is a flower
Of
Immense beauty
Let it
Unfold..."

(Poems from My Heart, 'Divine Lotus')

1 the journey begins

THIS IS THE STORY of a journey. A journey, that once begun, had to continue . . .

I was born into a religious family, the youngest of three girls. My father was born in Ranchi, India. He was the son of a civil engineer of Anglo-Irish descent and of the daughter of a highly placed administrator in the princely state of Kashmir. His family had lived in India for many generations. My father had been sent back from India as a jaundiced infant and had subsequently remained in England for his boarding education before training for the ministry. He was an Anglican clergyman with an enquiring mind and an unconventional approach to all matters religious.

My mother was the daughter of missionaries in Canada on her mother's side and of successful business people on her father's. She had an insatiable evangelical streak but she was also a visionary with a strong intuition. She was certainly very aware of another reality as well as this one. Mother also had an amazing sixth sense, especially when it came to certain people, which she would make sure we all knew about! She was a healer – with powerful, hot, healing hands. As a young woman, she had done a course in physiotherapy and was good at manipulating and massaging the many twisted ankles and sprained wrists that I sustained through messing about in the garden or when I was practicing gymnastics and cartwheels, which I loved doing. Maybe the world looked better upside down?

As you may have guessed, I was something of a tomboy and I often used to climb up into the big old trees that grew in our garden, and over the many hedges or fences, getting myself into a right old tangle! I was frequently to be found on one of the many rooftops of the old outbuildings which ran alongside what we all called the 'ash path'. It was the place where the hot ashes from the fire-places in the house would go once they had cooled down.

I loved exploring and had a 'den' which I thought nobody knew about. This was one of several secret places to which I disappeared if in trouble, which was a lot of the time! I had a rebellious spirit, that often reared its head when I felt unjustly accused.

Our family lived in a large, rambling old rectory full of mice and cobwebs, in a little village in the heart of Gloucestershire which was surrounded by beautiful hilly countryside. We had two dogs, a cat and six goats! It was a great place for a child to grow up.

There were several big fields which belonged to our rectory and at the far end of one, there was a huge, old oak tree that we kids called the 'Echo tree,' and when I stood under it, facing our house and shouted loudly, my voice would bounce back and forth several times! It was a favourite haunt of mine.

In the field next to the house, there was a small pond. Every Spring it produced thousands of tadpoles and I went every day to see how they were all growing. It was amazing how these little wriggly things could turn into mighty, greeny-grey speckled frogs leaping all over the place.

'Nature is remarkable,' I thought.

In this same field lived a large bull with tiny curls all over his huge forehead and he was my special friend. I called him Rajah as he was so mighty and kingly. He had such lovely big eyes with long black eye-lashes. I was not at all afraid of him and he was very intelligent.

From a very early age, I discovered that the world was a hard place to live in. So many sad things happened. The farm opposite our rectory was farmed by three brothers. They owned Rajah. After four years of seeing him nearly every day, he suddenly disappeared and was never seen again! It broke my heart. I am sure he was taken to the slaughterhouse. I didn't understand at the time why they had to take him away. Why? Why? It didn't seem fair. Yes, life was definitely most unfair.

I loved animals and felt strongly about animal rights. I used to save up my pocket money and send some of it to the Anti-vivisection Society. I hated seeing any living thing suffering and could see no justification in experimenting on animals for the so-called benefit of humans.

I was a very sensitive child. One day, I watched a very large tree being cut down. It was a huge, magnificent horse-chestnut, which had stood right in the middle of a field for many years, not far from where I went to school. I thought it was a terrible thing to do to such a beautiful old tree. It really broke my heart and I cried and cried for several days.

I loved going into the nearby woods and spent a lot of time there. Life at home was not easy so I would frequently go and find peace and quiet away from the claustrophobia of the rectory and the erratic discipline of my parents. They didn't have a lot of patience with me, especially when it came to the end of the school term and my class reports, having very high expectations of my academic progress. I hated school and was often bullied. The usual reason was just because my father was a vicar. I did not enjoy being a vicar's daughter at all. There was one part of the woods where beautiful bluebells grew in great abundance, and their smell was amazing. A narrow trail wove its way right through this particular bit of the wood and it was here that I frequently ended up. I loved it in this magical place and I felt really safe. These woods felt so 'alive'.

In the surrounding fields there were lots of rabbits and the air was thick with birdsong. Many wild flowers grew there and over time I became an 'expert' on all their different names and won a competition at school for a biology project where we had to collect as many different wild flowers as we could, press them and then display them on large sheets of paper complete with all their correct English names, Latin names, the dates and the places where we had found them. My parents really encouraged me in this project and if we were driving somewhere and I saw a flower on the edge of the roadside, my father would stop the car and I would climb out, pick it and take it home for my collection.

In the woods, I often 'heard' things other than the usual woodland noises and I could 'see' the various woodland folk. I never felt alone here and they became my friends. They were about as tall as I was, but then I was quite small!

Some of them were very beautiful and others had mischievous faces. I loved them because they laughed a lot. And they could really move fast, too. Some of them seemed to disappear right before my eyes and that always surprised me. They were all so young looking – rather like me – and they seemed to like my visiting them because when I approached the woodland, they made a sort of 'chattering' noise as if they were all talking at once. I spent many long hours there. I thought that everybody else could see them as well, but I found that they could not and I had to keep quiet about it or get badly teased. I could share this knowledge with my mother. She understood very well; she said that she could see them too. This was our little secret!

Sometimes, 'visitors' would come to see me when I was in my cot. I remember one particular occasion when a very tall lady with a long robe came and leant over me. She had long black hair and a beautiful face. She spoke softly to me and she felt very kind and loving.

From a young age, I was curious to know about other worlds, especially as I could see all these beings. I never seemed to be very much interested in what was going on in the 'real' world.

Our old rectory was haunted. Sometimes footsteps could be heard hurrying backwards and forwards along the narrow corridor that connected our huge front, stone stairway to the little wooden staircase which went right up the back of the house to two large attic rooms in the roof. Usually, we didn't take much notice of these odd sounds and nobody ever actually saw any of the ghosts. I often wondered why they continued to hang around the place.

I imagined all kinds of scenarios as to how they must have lived in the rectory all those years ago. I thought that ghosts liked inhabiting old and lonely places but this didn't seem quite true of our house as we were a pretty noisy lot! Sometimes if I was left alone at home, I would sit in the lounge with the long, iron poker in my hand, just in case they came to get me.

I was told that ghosts were the spirits of people who lived a long time ago and had died, not wanting to leave the place where they had been living. I often wondered if they were aware of their condition and whether they really knew that they were trapped in some kind of a time warp. I wondered if they could 'choose' to show themselves to us human beings or not and what it might feel like being a ghost. I imagined that it might be frustrating not having a real live body. Did ghosts come from the same place as the fairies, I wondered? It intrigued me that there could be so many other beings inhabiting the world as well as us.

It was in this old rectory with its beautiful, rural setting that we got to meet all kinds of people from many different walks of life. My parents were always interested in learning about other philosophies and religions. So, at their invitation, we had a constant stream of visitors to our home. People came from Europe and far away exotic places such as Africa and India. They were frequently well known in their particular field of knowledge, although I didn't fully appreciate this fact until I was somewhat older.

Writers, spiritual teachers and guides as well as clairvoyants and authorities on all kinds of weird and wonderful things found their way into our home. Some came to teach Vedanta philosophy whilst others gave lectures on the possible existence of UFOs and would discuss their various 'sightings'. Where did the UFOs come from? I was keen to know about it all. Demonstrations of all kinds of meditation techniques and various forms of yoga would be on offer to the different groups of people who gathered frequently in our lounge. Discussions would take place about all that was magical and mystical. I was particularly interested in the subject of 'past lives'. How many previous lives had I already had? How did they happen? I used to spend a lot of time wondering and my fertile young imagination would really go to town, thinking about what kind of a life I might have had last time round. I wondered in what exotic places I could possibly have lived and how did I get this life? Did I 'choose' it? Did I choose my parents? I was convinced that there was no way I could have 'chosen' my parents! Why would I want to come back anyway? Was it to 'learn' something? I had so many questions...

Some of the people who came to the house said that they could also 'see' fairies and other spirit beings. They said that these beings really lived in a 'dimension' other than our own physical world and not everybody had a talent to be able to know or 'see' them. They said that I was very lucky to have this skill, that it was a privilege and that these spirits and beings would only show themselves to those human beings with whom they felt safe and appreciated. I certainly appreciated them.

I loved meeting all these guests with their fascinating tales of their adventures and experiences. I was particularly drawn to the Indian visitors. They always seemed to have an aura of peace around them. I liked to try, in my own way, to meditate just as they did.

I remember one large, particularly interesting lady with wavy, red hair which she tied up in a sort of French roll. She was a regular visitor to our home and she said that she could see the fairies. She was an Irish countess. She wore very long, purple dresses. We three girls found it amusing when we went for walks with her, because when she bent down to climb underneath the barbed wire fences which separated the fields, she would invariably get stuck and we would have to unhitch her from all barbed spikes. She wore thick brown stockings that would slowly but surely wrinkle down to her ankles as the day progressed. She was a real eccentric and I liked eccentrics.

All these meetings fed my already receptive and extremely fertile imagination. The world offered me a kaleidoscope of infinite possibilities and I wanted to know about them all.

My mother used to call me the 'mystical' child to all these people. I didn't really know what she meant at the time, but it made me feel a little special.

Because of all these comings and goings at home, I grew up to be unprejudiced over race or colour and I always wanted to hear about other peoples' spiritual paths. People were people and I found them all to be a jolly fascinating lot!

Now, all these activities were the more exciting because they all happened in the 1950s — when opportunities for meeting such unusual people were extremely rare. I was indeed very fortunate.

2 an extraordinary man

IN THE EARLY DAYS, one special old man used to come to our home. He came on his own and each time he would stay for a few days. A tall and strikingly good-looking man, he was very gentle and quiet. He had an amazing shock of dark brown hair, tinged with a few golden strands, which grew down to his shirt collar, and a big, bushy beard. Over the years he was to become my dearest and closest friend. I loved him deeply and I knew that he loved me and I was always thrilled when he came to visit us. He used to tell me stories and he was also a fine artist. I thought he was the wisest person alive as he seemed to know the answers to just about everything!

I trusted him and always had lots of questions ready when he appeared. I knew that he would take the time and trouble to explain things to me. Whenever he spoke it was as if I was the only one who really mattered. That greatly impressed me. Nobody else spoke to me in such a caring way. He talked about many interesting things in such an easy manner that I could really understand. He knew so much about the different paths that people took in the quest for meaning in their lives. It didn't seem to matter whether these paths were from the East or from the West. He was a vast reservoir of knowledge and over these childhood years, he was to share many amazing things with me.

One day, we were out in the garden and he started talking. He said, that if I looked around hard enough, I would discover many things that were hidden away from my sight, but just because I couldn't see them, it was not to say that they didn't exist. All I had to do was imagine that I really could see them and not give up before I had given it a 'jolly good try'. He then produced a package that was tucked under his arm. It contained an oil painting he had done, which he had had mounted into a beautifully hand-carved frame. He held it up very carefully for me to see. First, he asked me to look and see how many little birds there were hiding in the painting, then to have a closer look and see how many different kinds there might be as well . . .

Immediately, I found myself looking at a most beautiful landscape with snow-capped mountains in the distance and a lake at the bottom which reflected them. Above, there was a lovely clear blue sky with several little white puffy clouds floating by. Two grey dappled horses were grazing just off centre in a field, just behind a small hedge with a long wooden farm gate in the middle of it. Some very tall, thin trees stood in the distance, reaching out towards the sky and there were several little birds flying high above them.

My mind went quiet as I began to concentrate . . .

He smiled gently at me, 'Well what can you see?' He turned it all into a beautiful game.

I continued to look very carefully and was surprised to find out how many birds there actually were. It was always an adventure with him. The more I looked, the more I began to see. The more intensely I looked, I began to see even more clearly. Slowly, one by one, all the little birds that were hiding away from my immediate view became visible. Some of them were sitting, hidden on the branches of the tall trees. There were a couple flying in the clear blue sky; three were cuddled up with just their little heads peering out of a nest that was deep inside the hedge and yet others were to be found hiding in the form of shadows that fell on the slopes of the mountains. I also noticed that there seemed to be five different kinds of birds . . .

He said, 'My dearest child, when you take the time to really look, you see that there is more to this picture than you could possibly have first imagined.' It was true. I was surprised at how so many birds could be so cleverly hidden away in this picture. We spent a long time together looking at it.

After a while, he put the picture down and said, 'Now look. Here is another view. Take a very close look at this.' He then proceeded to wave his arms all around him, sweeping around to the immediate view then he said, 'Here, you can see a magnificent garden with its lovely lawns from this little woodland. You can see all these beautiful flowers, the trees, the fallen leaves, twigs, the earth, the sky and the clouds, the birds . . . and look . . . just over there at that little squirrel with a large bushy tail . . .'

Then, he asked me something which I thought was very strange and mysterious. 'Now, can you see where the "me" and the "you" are, hidden away in this picture?' What did he mean? I thought to myself, and looked somewhat baffled, wondering what on earth he was talking about!

He smiled and repeated, 'Look very carefully all around you and see if you can see the "you" and the "me". I began to look around the garden. I wasn't at all sure what he was expecting me to say. Was he trying to trick me? Maybe, he was a little more crazy than I thought . . .

'I'm not sure I know what you mean!' I said. I quickly pointed at myself and then pointed to him.

'Well . . . no, no, no!' he laughed. 'It is not quite as simple as that. You see, there is actually no "you" or "me" here at all. Yet, at the same time, we are all these things.'

'What are you talking about?' I retorted, thinking that he had gone completely mad.

'Of course there is a you and a me! And how can we possibly be all these things as well?'

'Listen carefully, I'll let you into a little secret.' He half whispered to me in his most mysterious way that I was not what I thought I really was, but . . . actually, I was . . . something much, much greater than just this small child who was always asking loads of questions. I was really 'pure consciousness and pure awareness' — just the same as the trees, the woods and the birds and also the little squirrel . . .

'How can that be?' I asked, looking up into his kindly eyes and wrinkled face. I asked him if he was being serious and not just teasing me for these were big words and big ideas to a small child. I wanted to know so badly what he was talking about.

He chuckled. 'Of course I am being very serious. I would never tease you over such important things as these'. He continued, 'So, can you tell me what it is that makes a leaf green? a bee hum? that makes a rose smell? And what is it that makes the rain wet and the sun hot?'

I admitted that I could honestly say that I had never really given it a second thought. But, I thought that the conversation might be going somewhere interesting . . .

'Umm. Well, it has to be something that we can't see with our normal eyes,' I offered, trying to make some sense of this extraordinary conversation.

'Yes, sort of,' he said. 'It is something you may just be able to sense or you might "feel" very deeply within you. Pure consciousness and pure awareness is energy that is to be found everywhere and **in** everything. It actually **is** everything. It is the air we breathe and in the food we eat and some people may call this energy, "Source" or "God". It is that, which is you and me too. It is what you might call the raw fabric of the universe'.

'The raw fabric of the universe? What is that?' I asked.

'It is pure energy,' he repeated. 'You see, this is the secret, though it is not really a secret at all because *God* or *pure consciousness* is everywhere. For many centuries, only a few sages, seers and mystics seemed to know about this so-called mystery, this secret, as to what we really think we are made of and who we really are.'

I was curious, 'Why did the sages know this secret and not other people?'

This lovely old man, who was so knowledgeable sat down beside me on a log and looked far away into the distance. He was so peaceful. He was never impatient and always spoke very gently to me.

'Because the sages were consciously searching for God, they would spend all their time looking deeply within themselves for the meaning of life. They looked for meaning in all of their daily actions as well as in their meditations. They spent their whole lifetime doing just that. But ordinary people don't always have the time or the inclination to enquire or seek for this understanding. So they go and listen occasionally to preachers who sometimes mislead them.

'I guess what I am really trying to say is that the "you" and the "me" that we normally understand and know with our physical senses is . . . the **outside** bit of the inside. This "outside" is the bit that we are usually **only** interested in. But then, actually, we are not only the outside but also the inside.' Then he laughed and laughed and laughed. He continued laughing as he watched my incredulous face.

'The outside bit of the inside?'

'Yes, the "real" you and me is that bit which is . . .
the **inside** bit of the outside. That is the bit that you
don't get to see with your physical eyes and which is
the bit that we're not usually so interested in precisely
because we can't "see" it easily. But we are both the
outside of the inside and the inside of the outside and,
in fact, we should be as much interested in the inside
as we are in the outside! Actually, if we were really to
understand the inside, we would come to make sense
of the outside better. Then we would discover the
secret that it is all one and the same thing! This is the
truth.'

Then I started laughing too. I was beginning to
understand and 'sense' very gradually that maybe I
really was that very *energy* that the old man was talking
and laughing about, which made me who and what I
was and which made my lovely old friend who and
what he was. This was the secret . . . the secret of
knowing that we are not what we think we are, but
that we are really part and parcel of everything which
is manifested in the world around us. Was this also true
of the parts of my life that I didn't like?

'Yes, even those bits too.'

Hmm. I would have to think about that one! He
said he would tell me about that sometime.

I gave him a big hug and ran back into the house,
laughing and laughing. He always made me feel so
joyful. It felt good to be alive with him around. I
secretly hoped that he might talk to me again soon and
tell me more about who or what he thought I was.

3 lotus feet

OVER THE YEARS, my family were to meet several wonderful saints. One such was a very well known Sikh spiritual teacher, HH Sant Kirpal Singh, who travelled around the world, teaching people how to meditate. He often spoke with reference to Christianity as well as to other religions, showing the essential unity of all their spiritual teachings. When my parents and sister were initiated, I was very upset that they hadn't taken me along too. My parents had said I was too young but I really wanted to meet Kirpal Singh as I somehow 'knew' inside me, that he was a very special person.

We also came to know more about the Vedanta movement through meeting Swami Aviyektananda. He had been a devotee of Sri Ramakrishna, the saint who had lived near Calcutta (now known as Kolkata) in the late nineteenth century. Sri Ramakrishna sounded like a really amazing man, who had spent most of his days in blissful ecstasy due to his own spiritual practice and love for the goddess Kali. We used to visit Swami Aviyektananda at his home in Bath. I remember that he would save up all the Indian stamps from his old letters for me, as I used to collect stamps in those days. As a result, I had a huge collection of Indian ones! He also explained to me who the different people were on each of the stamps. He told me about the life and times of Mahatma Gandhi, who had tried to unite the peoples of India through passive resistance to British rule. Mahatma Gandhi's life and teachings really impressed me. He also talked about the different wild animals that were portrayed and how and where they lived in India. Swami Aviyektananda was a beautiful soul. He told me lots of amazing things about reincarnation and the many past lives I might have had as well as other spiritual topics.

Sometimes we were taken to visit another saintly Indian man, who was known to us affectionately as 'Nandi' or, sometimes, 'Nandiji.' He was married to a German lady and they lived in London with their three children. We used to like going to see them as the children were a similar age to us and we all got on well together. Nandiji was a very kind and gentle soul and many words of wisdom would fall like petals into my heart. My parents really loved and respected Nandi who was a very silent and peaceful sort of person and I loved the quality of stillness he possessed. I wondered how he managed to stay so placid when everything around him was not necessarily quite so calm!

As children, we were raised as vegetarians. Many of the people who visited our home were also vegetarian and my family belonged to a branch of the Vegetarian Society, which met in Gloucester. Even our family doctor and his two colleagues were vegetarian, which I think was quite unusual in those days.

Both my parents had a great affinity with India. India had been 'home' for the seven previous generations of my father's family although he didn't talk much about it with us children. In fact, it was not to be until I was quite a bit older that I came to know about our long family connection with India. I had always taken for granted liking the idea of India and Indian things. In fact, I felt quite 'Indian' myself and hoped that one day I would get the opportunity to visit this vast and enthralling country.

Once, dad sent away to India for our shoes. Mother first drew around our feet on various bits of brown paper then sent them to a place where the shoes were hand-made from leather taken from animals that had died of old age or other natural causes. Some months later, the shoes arrived. As you can imagine, they didn't fit very well. Our feet had grown so much during the long wait for them.

One day, a young Indian from North India who was a disciple of Sri Swami Rama of the Himalayas, came to our house and taught yoga, meditation and mysticism to those who were interested. My parents had met him through the Vegetarian Society. Usharbudh Arya was like a brother to me and he appreciated and loved coming to our home. We spent many happy hours together. He showed me how to climb trees bare-footed so I could get up faster and, at the same time, have a more secure foothold. He often ran around the garden with me on his shoulders and we had a great old time.

Usharbudh was a gentle, fun-loving person who had a tremendous knowledge of the Vedas. These teachings were awe-inspiring. He could chant beautifully in Sanskrit. The classical Indian way of chanting was beautiful and transported me to one of those special magical places locked away somewhere in my being. I loved Usharbudh greatly.

My parents had some old records of beautiful Sanskrit devotional chants and sometimes we would sing along with them. One was of some chants by an Indian saint called Paramahamsa Yogananda. A particular favourite has stayed in my mind: '*Hai Hari Sundara, Hai Hari Sundara, O God beautiful, O God Beautiful . . .*' I could see a vision in my mind's eye, of a vast ocean with the sun reflected in it just like melted gold.

4 light and shade

THE INTERESTING visitors to our home certainly made up for the lapses in so many other areas of my upbringing. Life was not easy for me or my two elder sisters. Dad, being a clergyman, expected us to be the best behaved of all children and we were always being dragged off to church for just about every service that was held. This included christenings, marriages and funerals. I would have to sing in the choir, ring the bell, take the collection or pump the organ so that the organist could play! Fortunately, our organist, Mr. Steele was a very good friend of mine because he loved nature just as much as I did and he used to like talking to me. He used to bring me treats and little boxes to keep my treasures in. He was a very kind man.

I loved music and studied the recorder and the violin at school. I played the violin in the orchestra and I got on well with the music teacher. Reading music was not one of my strong points, but if I listened very carefully to what was being played I found that I could play most of the parts by ear, and nobody was any the wiser! I also sang soprano in the school choir. I was always so excited and enthusiastic about the music classes that I spent a lot of time talking about them to the others and, as a result, I frequently got sent outside the door, which really upset me, but I just couldn't seem to help myself.

As a family, we often got together in the lounge to play music. It was compulsory. But fortunately, I enjoyed these sessions. Mother played the piano while dad and we three girls were each on the violin. Sometimes I played the recorder. A friend of my parents bought me a beautiful wooden treble recorder and I loved the deep, resonant and haunting sound it made.

I adored dancing. Whenever I had a chance, I would choose a piece of music from one of my favourite 78 rpm records and dance in front of any visitors who came to the house. I nagged and nagged my parents to let me go to ballet classes until they eventually gave in. The ballet school that I went to, put on quite a few shows and after a few months I did my first performance. It was a great occasion because I was dancing for the first time on my toes with my very first pair of pointe shoes. I felt like a real ballerina! At the ballet classes, I had a chance to meet other girls who shared this interest, which was great, especially as I was discouraged from bringing friends home to play with. I hadn't had many friends up to this point in my life but perhaps solitude was what pushed me into having such a creative and rich inner life and encouraged me to become interested in spiritual things.

However, as I could 'see' other beings and often found myself surrounded by them, I felt as if I was never really alone. I was a day-dreamer, an idealist who from a very early age could tune into the magic that seemed to be just about everywhere. Despite everything, I was always a very optimistic child. This quality kept me going through many a difficult time and I felt fortunate to have this capacity for 'bouncing back' into a more positive frame of mind.

We were raised with a great love for horses. Both of my parents had ridden for years and my aunt Mabel, my father's elder sister, had riding stables in Brixham. She had been born and raised in India, but when she eventually came back to England with my grandmother, they moved to South Devon.

Auntie Mabel was to run these stables for the rest of her life. I loved the smells of the stables with the mixture of hay and horses and I spent as much time as I could there. Every holiday that we spent visiting them, she would take us out riding to help exercise her horses and ponies. Sometimes, we went out to some really lovely places like Sharkham Point, which sadly has now become a housing estate.

And we always had a 'jolly good gallop' along the long, sandy beach of Mansands. Auntie Mabel taught us just all there was to know about caring for horses as she considered herself an absolute authority! She was very strict and always thought of the horses' welfare above all else. She loved each and every one of her horses as if they were her very own children. We all used to go to the local gymkhanas. Sometimes, we were lucky and won rosettes and prizes. Those were great moments.

As a girl, I was unaware of the sadness and hardship that had accompanied my grandmother's and aunt's return from the comparative ease of colonial life in India to the difficulties of making a living for themselves back in England. For me, visits to Brixham were happy occasions and my love of horses has remained ever since.

5 a lesson from the heart

ONCE, WHEN my old bearded friend was visiting, I asked him if he would walk in the garden with me as I had something to ask him. He was so wise and full of stories.

I said, 'You enjoy coming to our home and staying with us and we all love to see you. Especially me. Is having *attachment* for someone or something the same as "loving" them?'

I could think of many things that I loved and was greatly attached to. First of all, I loved this old man. I loved our two dogs and I had certainly loved Rajah and I missed him terribly now he had gone. I hoped that he had died peacefully and without too much suffering.

'Umm,' he said. 'Now that is a very interesting thought.' Then he went silent for a few moments before he spoke again. 'First of all, "attachment" to something or someone, is not necessarily the same as loving them. **Really** loving someone or something is very pure and comes from the heart. Attachment does not come from the heart. It comes from the thoughts and wishes that we all have, and these come from our head. That is, from our minds. And sometimes when we do love someone or we become "attached" to something else, we are also loving and being attached to **ourselves,** in a funny sort of way!'

40

I said, 'This sounds like something you once said to me: that we were not really separate, but that we were all somehow interconnected . . . '

'Yes, we are not separate really. When we truly understand that, it is easy to love without any attachment. It is because you think that I am a *you* and you also think to yourself that you are a *me*...that we feel the need to love somebody or something else, that we have all this confusion.'

I must admit I was extremely confused and my face must have shown it for he laughed and laughed. How I loved his laugh. There was much more laughter around the house when he was about. But he was always talking in riddles or so it seemed to me. I sincerely wanted to understand it all.

I said, 'But we are just a little bit separate aren't we? I mean, we are different. I am small and young, and you are big and old.'

'Yes, my dear, I am indeed old, but let me tell you something. Each one of us is a very small but important part of an immensely vast picture. Because we are seemingly so different, we think that we are "separate" instead of understanding that each one of us is really divinely connected to each other. We all have that divine spark within us. We are part and parcel of the whole picture.'

I was so fascinated by his smiling, shining face that I hadn't heard a single word he had said and had asked him to repeat it all over again. He roared with laughter! His laughter was contagious.

'Dearest child, when we think of ourselves as being different from others, we begin to get possessive and hang on to those things that are nearest and dearest to us. We say they are "mine" and belong to "me"; that they are our personal belongings; that we own them. Yours and mine. This is how we become "attached".

'You know it is not about whether we should or should not have certain things, or eat or drink certain things or do certain things that we love to do. The only thing we **do** need to do, is to give up our "attachment" to them because it brings us a lot of pain when we don't or can't have them.'

'But we would not love something or someone unless we felt attached to them, would we?'

His eyes grew a little misty and then he said, 'If we really do love each other, then we will **always** want the best for that person no matter what, regardless of our own personal wishes and choices. Do you understand that? To "love" someone does not necessarily mean that we have to be "attached" to them.'

'Yes,' I said.

We sat silently side by side for a little while. I really did love this old man and I certainly was terribly attached to him. 'Why?' I asked myself. I tried hard not to be! Ummm . . .

He broke my reverie with a very serious look and said, 'There is something else I would like to say to you about attachment. Sometimes we can be so attached to something that it can turn into an "addiction" and that can be very dangerous. Addiction is when we need something **so badly** we cannot live without it: like drinking lots of alcohol or taking drugs and not being able to stop. After some time, this kind of attachment would eventually make us ill. We may even be driven to stealing so that we can obtain more of the thing to which we are addicted. Our life would become a terrible mess as a result and lead us to great mental confusion. This kind of attachment is very serious. So we must be very clear and careful about our desires and needs.'

I was really shocked. Yes, I remembered that I had once seen an old, sickly-looking beggar sitting on the side of the road, drinking something which didn't look too good out of a dirty old bottle. He had looked in a very sad state. I started to wonder what it was that made people go and do such things...

'Why do people become addicted to things that harm them?'

My old friend looked a little sad and said, 'Sometimes, people who have had something really bad happen to them turn to drinking or taking strong drugs. It is a means of blocking out the pain of some deep-seated memory. They think that it is the only way of coping with their lives. This is a good example of how people can feel "separate" from others. Do you understand, my child?'

'Yes, a little,' I said, wondering how they could ever change things for the better once they got into this terrible situation. If we really were not separate from each other, then maybe somebody or something could help them?

6 life in the snow belt

WHEN I WAS fourteen, I emigrated to Canada with my parents, two dogs and my middle sister, Yvonne. My eldest sister, Heather didn't come with us and the break-up of our family made me very sad. We three sisters were not to meet up again until thirty years later, in much happier circumstances.

The old life was over and a new chapter full of possibilities was opening itself up to me. I was thrilled about the trip as we were going to travel on what was to be one of the last sailings of the SS Ivernia across the Atlantic. We sailed through great ice packs cutting and slicing our way through. It was really exciting. Every day, we went to see the dogs in their kennels, situated higher up on the ship and we gave them lots of hugs and walks on the wet, salt-sprayed wooden deck. They must have wondered what on earth was going on, but they kept pretty happy and healthy considering how everybody else, including some of the crew, was getting sick with the roller coaster journey and wild weather.

Schools of whales followed us for a lot of the way. Some of them were leaping right out of the water alongside the ship. They were so beautiful to watch.

When we reached Canada, we were the first ship to get up the St. Lawrence Seaway after the freezing winter months. Even so, we only got as far as Montreal as the river further upstream was still frozen solid. Eventually, we all disembarked into a very white, wintry world and we proceeded to Toronto by way of the Canadian Pacific railway. We had taken nine long days to reach our destination.

I loved Canada from the moment we landed. It was all so incredibly beautiful and everywhere there were pine trees heavily laden with snow. There was so much space and the snowy environment lent a special sort of silence to the surroundings. Here, I felt I could really breathe. I hoped that my parents could relax more and that life would be easier...

When we finally arrived in Markdale, ninety miles north of Toronto in the snow belt, I felt really at home. The Canadian people around us were very friendly and made us all feel so welcome. They had even filled our fridge and freezer with all kinds of delicious foods to help get us settled in. Our new home was a typical Canadian style house with a verandah along the front of it. The kind of verandah one used to see on television in the old American movies, where the elderly folks were to be seen relaxing in their rocking chairs reminiscing about the 'good ol' days'!

The house was large and had a fair sized garden with an old apple tree to one side of it. Rumour had it that a long time before, a maid had hung herself from it. How sad. We never found out why. It seemed that wherever we lived, there was always an accompanying ghost!

We had a couple of beautiful maple trees in the front garden and two young boys who lived just opposite, showed us how to 'tap' the maple syrup from them. This maple syrup was delicious – especially on pancakes along with piles of cream!

My parents enrolled me at the local school and I was really happy for the first time in my school life. The teachers were kind and I made many friends there.

This was a new experience for me. I was not bullied and so I was able to relax more and work harder at my studies.

Once we had settled down, I wanted to continue going to dance classes, but the nearest ballet school was in Owen Sound which was twenty-five miles away. There was no way that my parents would take me that far so I decided to start my own school. Dad allowed me to set up some classes on Saturday mornings in the church hall, in the basement of the church. This project was a great confidence builder and quite a few children came to the classes. I taught them everything I knew. My mother came in one day during one of these classes and she was quite surprised to see how well they were going. The kids were really enjoying themselves. I loved all the children who were so enthusiastic.

I got to know a boy at school who was in grade thirteen and we became good friends. He was a very talented pianist and I talked him into coming and playing the piano for my twenty or so, students. He was very chuffed when I paid him. At age fifteen, that was a funny feeling – employing someone! I felt empowered and my confidence grew considerably. I was beginning to feel that I had some worth.

I enjoyed choreographing my own shows and took the students to perform regularly in the hospital and the local Old People's Home. This brought a lot of pleasure to everybody. The old folks really enjoyed seeing all the little children dancing. Some of my students were not so much younger than I was, yet we all got along really well together. Some of them were becoming good dancers, developing a great love and respect for the dance. I heard much later that at least one of the students had gone on to pursue ballet as a career.

Life in Canada was great. I was so much happier and felt fulfilled. I was the only child living at home now as my elder sister had gone to Toronto to college to train as a primary school teacher.

My parents were less strict and I had more freedom until it came to Sundays! They still insisted on involving me in the various activities of the church: like teaching Sunday school, which I didn't enjoy at all! I can't imagine what I taught the kids. I had no choice as to whether I should be there or not. I was very resistant. But it was out of this very resistance that I became more interested in doing my own spiritual investigation. After all, I thought, my parents had introduced me to all those other religions and philosophies back in England which had seemed much more interesting. Now I wanted the opportunity to explore them all in my own way and in my own time.

I had never ever enjoyed going to church except when the church was candle lit which created a beautiful atmosphere. There seemed to be so much hypocrisy most of the time. Here in Canada, people seemed to be more sincere, which helped. There was one church activity I did enjoy and that was belonging to the Anglican Young Peoples' Association (AYPA). There were lots of young people involved in this organisation. It was good fun going away on camps and meeting others from all around the place and singing together.

However, one day I decided to go and visit the Catholic church with one of my friends. It was right next door to our church. I wanted to know what all the differences were and why. My father was not at all pleased about this visit when he found out!

The Catholic church fascinated me. They had lots of rituals which I wanted to know about. There were candles everywhere which gave a beautiful peaceful atmosphere and the interior decoration of the church was bright with its many statues of the various saints as well as wall hangings. The smell of incense added to my curiosity. The atmosphere seemed to transport me to another place...

I liked the idea of using a rosary, to say special prayers to communicate with God, who, I felt, was much greater than we could possibly imagine. Later, I bought myself a beautiful turquoise rosary and wore it around my neck. It made me feel more connected to the divine in a funny sort of way.

In a corner of this church, was a large, painted statue of Mary, the mother of Jesus, and the people said special prayers particularly to her. The Catholics considered her to be divine and I was fascinated by the thought of praying to a woman to help us in our daily life. And why not? It was all very different from what was usually done in our church which was so uninspiring.

In our small town of Markdale with its one thousand or so inhabitants, there were no less than five different denominations of Christian churches. The Church of Canada was opposite our church and the Church of the Nazarene, Presbyterian, and the Methodist churches were just down the road. I couldn't understand why they needed to have so many Christian churches in such a small place.

Once, I went with my parents to visit the Anglican Convent of St. John the Divine in Toronto. The nuns were in the middle of vespers when we arrived. The sound of their Gregorian chanting in the chapel was absolutely heavenly. I was so inspired by this beautiful, spiritual atmosphere that, for quite a while afterwards, I seriously thought about becoming a nun. If I could spend the rest of my days chanting and praising the words of God, I would be very happy.

Sadly, our stay in Canada was to be a short-lived experience and we re-emigrated to England within a couple of years. My father didn't much like the combination of extremely cold winters and very hot summers. I was dragged back along with one poor dog—the other had died—leaving behind Yvonne who had fallen in love with Paul, a tall, handsome Canadian whom she eventually married.

I had no desire to leave Markdale. I was very happy there and had finally felt settled. I had many friends and had found a beautiful and good place in which to live. I was devastated. And what about all my ballet students? My studies were going so well for me in my Canadian school and the thought of going back to school in England was a total nightmare to me.

Two weeks before leaving, I went to visit a friend for dinner on her parents' ranch. She had a super carthorse who was strong enough to carry both of us. Before dinner, we got on this horse and she proceeded to show me around the place. At one point we went too close to a large farm gate, and I somehow managed to catch my leg on the side of it and fell off. I was seriously concussed, and was rushed off to hospital right there and then. No dinner! Seven stiches were put in the back of my head and I spent the last ten days in Canada in a hospital bed with terrible headaches and a suspected fracture of the skull. What a way to end my stay there. I really didn't want to leave.

7 the swinging sixties

I WAS SIXTEEN when we moved back to England, to a parish near Warminster in Wiltshire. My father took over two churches. I quite liked our new house. It was fairly big and old, set in very nice grounds with countryside all around. I kept a horse on a large part of the lawn that dad had kindly fenced off, just for her. She was a bright little Welsh Cob called 'Peggity' and very obedient. I adored her. Slowly, I came to terms with having to be back in the UK and settled down to my new life. I soon made some good friends in the area. I rode out regularly, exploring the surrounding countryside with one particular friend who lived and kept horses in the next village. She knew loads of young people in the area and introduced them all to me. My social life started looking up and I was invited to a few balls and cocktail parties. I had great fun racing around the country lanes with friends in flashy sports cars. The thought of becoming a nun had completely left my mind!

School proved to be as horrendous as I expected it would be. To start with, I found that age-wise, I was two years older than everybody else, having missed two years of course work. After attending an Anglican girls' convent for one year and then a grammar school for a second year, where I played hockey for the 1st eleven and did a lot of sport, I somehow managed to get into Salisbury College of Art on the strength of a portfolio which I had put together with my art teacher. I started on a foundation course having left school with very little else to show for the years of pain.

Art school was a place where I began to discover my potential: my place in the greater scheme of things. I was freer to a greater degree. Here, there were no expectations, apart from doing my work as well as I could. I found expression for that aspect of myself that was deeply buried within me. I made some good friends and we had a lot of fun together. This was a time of growing into maturity.

I enjoyed being an art student but I really craved more independence. I was tired of the claustrophobic and dictatorial environment which still dominated my home life. In Canada, my parents had been far more relaxed. Back in England, they reverted to a much stricter regime at home which made it pretty impossible to spend time with friends. I was already nineteen years old!

Eventually, I moved to London, to an International Christian Students' Centre in Earls Court which was a 'live-in and work' situation, which my parents had found for me. The job was as a cleaner and bed changer there along with other young people. I didn't enjoy the work at all, but I did get to meet a lot of interesting people from around the world. I made friends with some really beautiful Sunni Muslim Indians from East Africa, who were staying there. They were very warm and friendly and were happy that I was interested in learning about their culture. They frequently invited me out with them and spoiled me enormously with their delicious Indian snacks. They gave me several beautiful saris and showed me how to wear a sari properly. It was such a graceful garment and I felt very comfortable wearing one. They took me to their mosque and introduced me to their friends. I found their ceremonies, chants and prayers very beautiful and interesting. As things happened, they explained to me what was going on. It was extraordinary, listening to a different kind of music and experiencing very similar feelings to those that I had had when visiting the Anglican Convent in Toronto and listening to the nuns' chanting. It was so uplifting.

I recognised how much I loved the spiritual life in its various shapes and forms. In fact, I felt quite at home in the very different spiritual groups in which I happened to find myself. The truth seemed to be hidden in every church or religious organisation. I could see sincerity and hypocrisy sitting side by side. I had a longing in my heart for something that would be really meaningful to me, but I still only had a vague idea of what I thought that might be.

Whilst living in this Centre, I developed a mild form of tuberculosis and was ill for three months. I had many visions during this time and spent most of it in a blissful and very beautiful place. My Swiss room- mate kindly looked after me as it took quite a long time to get my strength back.

One day, I bumped into one of my old friends from art school days. I got to hear about the old crowd and what they were all doing. It turned out that one of them was living in a shared house just off the Kings Road, beyond the World's End Pub. I was tired of living and working in the Christian International Centre and they had a spare room which they offered to me. I was delighted.

It was an amazing place. Over a period of a few weeks, we would come home to find that all our beds had been messed up and the drawers were opened wide, with all the things chucked around the place. Would you believe it? This house was haunted by a poltergeist! We knew this because nothing was ever stolen.We tried to get rid of it by 'talking' to it and it did seem to quieten down for a while, but I don't think we ever quite got rid of it. We often had friends come around and we spent many a long night discussing ghosts and other mysterious and magical happenings. It was in this house that I was to meet my future husband, Godfrey. We immediately liked each other. He was tall, dark and handsome and a keen oarsman. A lot of our entertainment consisted in visits to the river Thames and attending the various regattas. We had a lot of fun together and he was different from the others I knew. He was serious as well as good fun. I liked his gentle nature. After five months, we parted. I was not yet ready to settle down to a long-term relationship . . .

Living in London was exciting. It was the 'Swinging Sixties' and there was a lot happening. I enjoyed being part of the hippy scene and had got myself a job working in a posh clothes boutique just off Sloane Square. Occasionally, I modelled evening dresses on the catwalk which was good money. For a while, life was fun as we spent most of the evenings going out to the psychedelic night clubs and getting invited to various grand balls and cocktail parties in and around London. It wasn't long before I got bored with this fast, shallow life and moved out. My parents had gone to the outskirts of Bristol to another parish and so I decided to move to Bristol too.

I got myself a job working as a commercial artist and loved it. Unfortunately, over a short period of time all the artists were made redundant and the work went elsewhere. So I started doing temporary office jobs here and there.

Life in Bristol was calmer and I began to look around for some spiritual nourishment. I had made friends with some Jewish people and discovered where the local liberal synagogue was. I began studying modern Hebrew and the Torah and I embarked on an intensive search into the teachings of Judaism. Each Sunday, I went to 'shule' at the rabbi's house. Going to the synagogue was a most interesting experience and I loved the chanting of the ancient prayers. I was again moved by sacred music. After a couple of years of deep soul searching and involvement with Judaism, I still did not find that inner peace in my life. I found it all far too patriarchal for me and the rabbi could not really answer my questions. Eventually I left.

Secretarial work was boring and I didn't see myself working in offices for the rest of my life but it did pay the bills! I had always been interested in the theatre so I auditioned for a semi-professional drama group which met regularly. It was good fun. Eventually, I auditioned for the Bristol Old Vic Theatre School. I thought that I might like to become an actress.

I met lots of interesting people in the theatre world, and fell in and out of love, until one day . . .

faith in life

"Twisting
And
Turning
In Love's
Sweet Embrace
Entwined
As One
The Universe
Sings
Her song"

(Poems from My Heart,
'Love's Sweet Embrace')

8 newly weds

WHILST SITTING in a boring old office in the centre of Bristol, I was chatting to the girl opposite me about a certain young man I had met in London. There and then, I decided to get back in touch with Godfrey. I really wanted to see him again. I knew that he had taken a year out of university to go and teach at a Lycée in Caen, France before taking his final exams. So, I rang his university, got his French telephone number, and rang him. When we made contact, I was surprised and delighted that he wanted to see me. Little did I know that he had *really* fallen in love with me the very first time we'd met. Once together again in France, it felt as if we had never parted. A month later we got engaged and ten months later we were married. Godfrey is still my strength and helpmate after thirty-five years of marriage.

We moved to Warwickshire where Godfrey finished his final year at university. Dreams of becoming a director or actress faded into the dim distance as I immediately became pregnant with our first child. Godfrey was a poet and a lover of both English and French literature which he often shared with me. I found great inspiration in the poetry of Baudelaire and Edgar Allan Poe. It stimulated my mind. There was so much creativity and innovation happening all around and people were looking for a new vision of hope in the world. The sixties were unlike any decade that had gone before.

About five months into my pregnancy, I had an extraordinary experience. At the time, Godfrey was studying hard at home as his final exams were looming ahead and I was working as a secretary. As I was going off to work I slipped and fell down quite heavily. I picked myself up and staggered back into our little flat and lay down on the bed. Godfrey was in the kitchen making me a cup of tea. The next thing I knew, there was a small boy of around two years old, standing beside me, stroking my brow and as he did so, he said, 'It's going to be all right, it's going to be all right.' I was deeply touched by this experience and knew in that moment, that I was going to have a little boy. He was 'visiting' me to let me know that all would be well! Little did I know how difficult his birth would actually be.

Godfrey graduated and got a job working as a trainee manager in the industrial world of paper packaging in Stevenage. So, we moved out of our quiet student accommodation, a small flat in the village of Ashow, near the university, and moved all our belongings to Stevenage. This included Solly, a lively Dalmatian puppy we had acquired from one of Godfrey's university friends who bred race horses and dogs! The house we moved to was a pretty noisy, chaotic place full of guys. Fortunately, the stay there was only temporary.

My pregnancy was not easy. When I went to the hospital for my six-month check-up, I was not allowed to return home and had to remain in the hospital, as there were some problems which needed checking out. The doctors informed me that I would have to have my baby induced sooner than expected. Neither of us was prepared for this news.

After a few days, I was given a general anaesthetic to have the delivery by Caesarian section, but came out of the anaesthetic — still with the bump! They told me that it was better to have the baby naturally, if possible. This time was difficult for me psychologically and for poor old Godfrey, who had just started his first job, driving daily from Stevenage to visit me in Bedford Hospital. It was a tiring journey for him after a day's work.

Finally, a month later, our son Nicolas was born, nine weeks premature. He was a very tiny, beautiful being who had a lovely mop of dark hair on his head. We were both thrilled. He was adorable but very underweight so immediately he was rushed into the intensive care unit where there were quite a few little babies being cared for. I was pretty distraught as I was in another ward and didn't want to be separated from him. It wasn't natural. At no time was he allowed out of the glass incubator, so I could not even have a cuddle with him. I also felt terrible physically as I had had lots of stitches which became infected and I could hardly walk. When I was able to move a little bit, I could only look at my little baby through the glass of the incubator. It all felt so inhumane.

Eventually, I was allowed to go home, leaving our little son behind, where he had to stay a couple more weeks until he had reached a better weight. Every day we went to the hospital to visit and feed him. Three and a half weeks after his birth, when he had just about doubled his weight, little Nicolas came home. We had just bought our first house, which was an end-terraced cottage up a country lane in a small village in the heart of the Bedfordshire countryside. Now we could begin our new life as a family with our little boy.

Life became meaningful and challenging, having Nicolas home with us. He was a very bright little chap. Fortunately, he had a good appetite and he began to grow quite quickly into a strong, healthy little lad. After a few weeks, I developed chronic back trouble and trying to run the home in this state with a a new baby was difficult.

Solly, our pup, loved little Nicolas. In fact, he thought he could 'mother' him! His one fault was that he needed so much exercise. Nicolas was also very demanding in his own way and it was becoming more and more difficult for me to cope with everything as I could hardly move. So we found another home for the dog. I was very sad at having to part with him. Gradually, my back improved.

After a few months, Godfrey got fed up with the packaging industry and decided to get into teaching. His father had been in education, so he had initially felt that he should do something else, but then he realised that education was his real vocation. He scanned the educational papers and got his first teaching job at a Village College in Cambridgeshire.

5 in the fens

WE SOLD OUR first house and moved into cheaper, rented accommodation provided by the school. It was pleasant enough and we all settled down happily and made some interesting friends.

At the school, we met a most unusual lady. She was the music teacher and everybody adored her. She was quite a heavy smoker and even smoked while she taught. She used to sit the ashtray on the top of the piano and the vibration of her playing would eventually knock the ashtray down into the piano's inner workings. Then there would be a great commotion while she bent over the piano, searching for the ashtray and itinerant fag-end. At the same time, revealing her splendid red, flannel knickers for everyone to see!

There wasn't anyone in her village who did not know her. She lived in a most beautiful thatched cottage with eighteen cats. As you can imagine, the place was very smelly! We got to know her really well as I always loved an eccentric! She was a clairvoyant and read the *I Ching*, an ancient Chinese fortune-telling classic. I was really fascinated to know more about it so I put up with the smell of cats, cigarettes and the chaos all around to learn all I could from her. She welcomed me in like a long lost friend and thus began my studies into the inner workings of this great classic work. It is a most interesting treatise and there have been several translations of it. Godfrey found it interesting too and bought me a copy of John Blofeld's book *The Book of Change*. The readings always proved to be very illuminating.

One day, this lady accidentally burned her house down. Most likely with one of her cigarette ends! The whole village clubbed together and had it totally refurbished for her, to a most beautiful design which included a wooden minstrel's gallery. They also bought her a spanking new grand piano. This really showed how much the local people appreciated her.

As I grew stronger after having Nicolas, I decided to go back to dance classes to train as a ballet dancer and teacher. Godfrey was very supportive and encouraged me to go.

This, I guessed, was probably the secret to successful partnership, allowing one another space to develop in our own unique way in order to become complete human beings. It certainly worked for the two of us.

Fortunately, I passed my driving test the day before I was due to start studying under the famous classical ballet teacher, Nina Hubbard, who had a large, well-known school in Cambridge. She had been a soloist with the Russian Kirov Company, in her day, and had married an Englishman after the war. I was a full-time student and had found a really nice baby sitter who also had a little boy. So, off I went to Cambridge every weekday afternoon. Now I was able to continue my training as a dancer even though it was such a long time since I had taken lessons.

Nina Hubbard was very strict and I knew that she was the very best I could possibly have. I felt very fortunate. She really encouraged me and I blossomed under her training. So, whilst working hard as a professional dance student and trainee teacher, I set up and ran my own ballet school, putting children through their dancing exams and did a lot of shows The students were so keen and enthusiastic. Godfrey also loved the ballet and was helpful when it came to booking the venues and organising the seating and ticketing arrangements for these events.

Godfrey was ambitious and he soon started to look for a more challenging job. He got a promotion to a new Sixth Form College in the Isle of Ely. So we moved to this very beautiful cathedral city and bought our own house. It was fun setting up a new place that also had a small garden where Nicolas could play. Godfrey was enjoying the challenge of his new job and we made friends easily around us.

We soon met a young couple who had two little children. They were all vegetarian. The husband was an English teacher and his wife had been a ballet dancer, trained at the same place as me. She was very artistic and she designed and made dresses, then sold them to friends and at markets. Once, she made some dance costumes for one of our annual school shows. The couple were Companions of the Druids. These esoteric teachings rather appealed to us and so we went to some fascinating meetings which were being held in Dulwich. Druidism intrigued me. It presented a different and more natural way of being.

Another couple we got to know had three young children and our six kids spent a lot of time together. This other friend was qualified to teach young children as well as being a music and movement specialist so I invited her to come and teach my baby ballet class, which she did brilliantly. She had the gift of much patience. If one child wanted to go to the toilet, then the whole class usually wanted to go too! But this never fazed her and they all adored her.

Our social life consisted of cooking the most delicious 'veggie' dinners together in each other's homes, and listening to psychedelic music. The kids slept all together upstairs. These were good times.

We planned for a second child: a little brother or sister for Nicolas and later, I gave birth to another little boy. Charles was born four years after Nicolas, pretty much on time in a really delightful and friendly little nursing home in Ely. The midwife was married to one of Godfrey's work colleagues and the nurse was a parent of one of his pupils. It was a bit of a family affair! The sad thing though was that this nursing home was going to be shut down for economic reasons. There were just two of us mothers left and as soon as our babies were born we got our photographs in the local paper to mark the home's closure.

I had kept pretty healthy during this pregnancy and was able to continue teaching dance right up to the last minute. I had found a young dancer to continue running the classes until after the birth. Once I was home, I took Charlie to the classes in his carry-cot, where he slept most of the time.

When the boys were older, they both joined the ballet classes, but it was not always easy teaching one's own children. They thought that they could do just as they pleased, as it was only 'mum' teaching!

We spent several happy years in Cambridgeshire until eventually Godfrey got a job in education administration in Hertfordshire so we bade farewell to all the parents and children of my ballet school and headed south.

10 finding community

WE SOON SETTLED down and I set up some new ballet classes in one of the local school's main hall. I had quite a lot of students and we started to give shows and do examinations. We found a fabulous little play group for Charlie, which was run by one of my 'ballet mums.' He was really happy there. Brenda (Auntie Frienda, as he called her) who ran it also loved him. Nicolas went to a local school, but he was not at all happy. It was obvious that we would have to try and sort something else out for him.

In the meantime, we started to look around for some sort of spiritual life that we could share together as a family. It was not possible to keep going to London for the Druid gatherings. We wanted something nearer home that the children could also be involved with as they grew up which would be meaningful and fun. We looked into the possibility of becoming Catholics, as I had enjoyed many aspects of the Catholic Church when I was younger. So we invited the local Roman Catholic priest around with a view to joining his church. His perspective on life and spirituality were so vastly different from where we were coming from, so we enquired no further in that direction. I felt sure that there must be something 'out there' for us, so we continued our search . . .

In the Seventies, folk music was very popular and we both enjoyed listening to local bands playing. One night, we went to a folk club in Hemel Hempstead old town where a talented young couple were playing flute and guitar. I was spellbound by their music. The flute and the guitar went so beautifully together. I was inspired to get back into playing music myself and decided to learn to play the flute. So, that Christmas, Godfrey bought me a really beautiful instrument and one of those 'teach yourself' books and gradually I began to master a few tunes.

Once again, I developed more problems with my back and was eventually admitted into the dancers' clinic at Guys Hospital in London. Whilst there, I met a young Indian woman who had had long-term back problems. She had been bedridden for some time and could barely walk. I was so sorry for her, but she was very philosophical about it all. She had been a professional Indian classical dancer.

We became good friends as we discussed our various dance backgrounds. I was thrilled to hear about her Indian classical dance. It had been a childhood dream of mine, ever since seeing a dance performance on the television, that I might have an opportunity to learn it one day. More immediately, I had to get myself well and ready to do the choreography for a professional pantomime at the Pavilion in Hemel Hempstead.

Godfrey met many interesting people in the course of his administrative work and whilst I was laid up in hospital, he met someone who was involved in teaching Travellers' children. She was a member of the Bahá'í Faith. Godfrey was immediately interested. The Bahá'í Faith seemed to be a religion that was not at all exclusive and embraced the whole of humanity. A world religion. This intrigued me, for over the years I had searched into so many different spiritual teachings, looking for real meaning in my life. Godfrey borrowed some Bahá'í books which he brought into hospital for me to read. He was really enthusiastic about it and wanted to find out more. Once I was back home, we went along to some of the meetings that they held regularly called 'firesides'. There were also some children's classes being held, so there was something interesting for the boys too.

We started going to some gatherings in Hemel Hempstead, and became Bahá'ís in February, 1977. It was exciting being involved in what seemed to be a dynamic and friendly international community of people who had a tremendous world vision. A vision of peace, of 'unity in diversity'. This was something really inspirational and wonderful. There were many children within the community and our two boys made lots of friends from all over the world.

We met a wonderful couple, Yvonne and Charles Macdonald. Charles was on the National Spiritual Assembly of the United Kingdom. We became very close friends and in particular I found a wonderful father figure in Charles. He had been a famous bomber pilot in the Second World War and his roots lay in Ireland and the Isle of Skye. He was full of stories which were very inspiring. His tremendous knowledge of the Faith inspired me.

A year later, my back started to play up yet again. I was in real trouble and had to go back to the hospital in London. An interesting thing happened on the night before I left for the hospital. We were staying at the home of the person who had first introduced us to the Bahá'í Faith. I was lying on the bed, and my back was locked in pain. I could not get into any comfortable position. I thought to myself, 'If I concentrated hard enough on Abdu'l Bahá, (the son of the founder of the Bahá'í Faith), maybe the pain might go away,'

Suddenly, I saw a beam of light and a Bahá'í symbol 'The Greatest Name,' manifested itself bathed in the light. It was very small and distant to start with, gradually getting bigger and bigger as it moved towards me. Then it seemed to 'melt' into me, and a wave of healing light went right through my body. This wave of light went through me several times and each time the pain in my back grew less and less until it was completely gone. It was most extraordinary. A miracle! After this I really did believe in miracles and I had a pain-free night.

This time I was in hospital for six long weeks and I woke up one morning to find that I was completely paralysed down the left side of my body. This was a terrible shock. I saw my whole life shattering before my eyes. I would never be able to dance again let alone do anything else. I visualised myself spending the rest of my life in some sort of terrible physical state. I thought about how unjust and cruel life was as the tears streamed down my face.

'Why me?' I wondered. I was so angry and bitter, but that did not help. I spent the whole day thinking about how I could come to terms with this condition...'I may be on my back for the rest of my life...' Oh my God! For a few hours I lay in a very dark place as I reviewed my options...

Gradually, a sense of calm overtook my thoughts and I decided that I would try not to be miserable about it any more. Life had to move on. I would accept my lot and make a new life for myself with my family. There would be constraints and difficulties, but we could work it all out. It would be a great challenge but I knew that I had a loving and supportive family whatever the outcome. So, little by little, I began to relax and let go of all this thinking...eventually I dozed off . . .

Twenty four hours later, the paralysis had gone as quickly as it had come. How strange! After this event, I was changed. I would never take anything for granted ever again. 'Nothing is ever certain in this life.'

Eventually, we moved from Hemel Hempstead, to Rushden in Northamptonshire, and we found a better school for Nicolas. He was much happier and Charles went to the local nursery school which was just round the corner from where we lived.

We joined the local Baha'ís in the area and discovered a really warm and friendly couple who had a farm near St. Neot's where they regularly held picnics. About a hundred or so Bahá'ís would gather together for these spontaneous events, just like one big, happy family. There were all kinds of activities going on for both the adults and the children. There were discussion groups, singing and devotional activities alongside cart rides and jumping in the hay. We got to know quite a lot of people through these events and the kids had a great time. This, we felt, was the ideal way to bring up a young family, with such a loving and strong community around us. In fact, we found that wherever we went, the local Bahá'is were always pleased to meet us just as if they were our family members.

It was not long after we had become Bahá'ís, that we were invited to the wedding of a beautiful Persian girl whom I had first met when she came to my dance classes. As a young girl she had been trained at the Royal Ballet School, so it was great to have her in the class. The wedding was extraordinary: simple yet beautiful and dignified. There was chanting in Persian and Arabic, which was so uplifting and Godfrey was asked to read a prayer in English. After the intimate family wedding there was a large reception and I suddenly caught sight of a very dignified, elderly lady who was sitting in a corner of the marquee. I was never backward in coming forward if I wanted to meet somebody so I went over and started talking to her, little realising that she was Ruhhiyih Khanum, the widow of the Guardian of the Bahá'í Faith whose resting place is in London. She was very kind and took no offence at my presumptiousness.

Some time later, we agreed to act as guardians for a young Persian girl who came to live with us. Mandana became like one of the family and she was especially close to little Charles, helping me to look after him. Mandana's parents had gone back to their home in Teheran in July 1979 just a few weeks before the outbreak of the Islamic Revolution. This meant that they could no longer leave the country. She was left with no family in England to care for her and so we took on the responsibility.

Mandana was great fun to be with, and we often went on shopping trips together. Whilst shopping in Bedford, we twice saw Ruhiyyih Khanum and we stopped to speak to her. She had remembered me from the wedding, not surprisingly. Later she sent a beautiful little note together with rose petals taken from the shrine of the Bab on Mount Carmel in Israel.

After three years in Rushden, we moved to Kenilworth taking Mandana with us and we continued enjoying Bahá'í community life. We held lots of events in our own home. One event was a Naw Ruz (New Year) party where a hundred and fifty people squeezed into our lounge. It was in the papers.

Godfrey was now working as a deputy-head in a large comprehensive school in Coventry, not far from where we were married.

In May 1981, our family went on Bahá'í pilgrimage to Haifa. We were really excited about the trip and I fell in love with the land of Israel the moment we arrived. There was such a cosmopolitan feel about it.

Haifa is a beautiful city and the atmosphere around the shrines seemed to be charged with a most amazing spiritual energy. It was intoxicating. Here, I felt close to God.

Charles, who was only six at the time and who had suffered a lot with asthma from birth, started having a particularly bad attack, possibly due to the change in the climate. We were very anxious and unsure as to whether to take him directly to hospital or risk going on the scheduled trip to the Shrine of Bahá'u'lláh. We decided on the latter course of action. In the hour that we spent in this most beautiful and heavenly shrine, Charlie became completely cured. It was a miracle and he was really impressed! He was never to forget that experience.

Amongst the visitors on pilgrimage, we met a delightful couple of American teachers who were working at a famous international Bahá'í school in Maharashtra, India. The wife had been a dancer with the Martha Graham Dance Company in America and one evening, the two of us went to watch a dance movie in the centre of Haifa. This couple spoke of a school that had high moral values and their aim was to educate students there into helping to bring about a new world order of peace, love and unity for humanity. It was an awesome project and we were very interested, particularly Godfrey as he was an educator first and foremost. They said that the National Spiritual Assembly (NSA) of the Bahá'ís of India were looking for some new staff members. Many students came from around the world to attend this famous school. We both felt that the mixing of diverse cultures would be a great education just in itself and that it was a unique opportunity for us and our children. So on our return home, we contacted the school. They were very interested in us and, after some time, we were invited by the NSA of India to join the staff of New Era High School in Panchgani.

How exciting! I had always wanted to go to India, and now the chance had come. So, in 1982 we sold up our home and furniture, gave a whole load of stuff away and off we went. What a wonderful way to clear out the old and lessen our load of possessions.

11 ā nᴇꞷ ᴇrā

INDIA IS AMAZING. The sights, the smells, the sounds were intoxicating. I was so happy to be there. Here I found my natural, spiritual home, and felt comfortable right from the very start.

Godfrey became Vice-Principal at New Era High School and I taught English as a Second Language and Moral Studies. It was the first time that I had ever done any classroom teaching. Most of the time, I enjoyed the experience. The children were keen to learn and were enthusiastic in the discussions we had on how to become better members of society. One book I used, was the story of *Jonathan Livingstone Seagull* by Richard Bach. The kids really loved it. It was so full of analogies to the human condition and needs.

We began our new home life in the upstairs part of a exceedingly spacious Dak bungalow. It was situated in beautiful grounds a couple of kilometres from the main school campus.

Not far away was a large and very beautiful Gulmohur (Flame of the Forest) tree, known for its bright red flowers. Life was made more interesting by having a pair of cobras living nearby. One day, Charles came face to face with one of the cobras as he returned from school. The king cobra raised his hood but rather than show a clean pair of heels, Charles just stood and gazed at the cobra who eventually tired of the

encounter and slid quietly away into the undergrowth.
When Namu, one of the servants living below us got
to hear about Charles's meeting with the cobra, he
couldn't stop explaining to us what good fortune it was.
Perhaps Charles's subsequent charmed life has had
something to do with this incident!

All the floors of our house were made of marble,
which was a luxury we came to look upon as a necessity,
because they were cool to walk on. The intense heat
outside was almost unbearable most of the time. A
grand balcony overlooked the main driveway where
one could see spectacular views of the great Western
Ghats. It was from this balcony that Kripa, our elderly
ayah, would often give us a regal wave as if she were
the memsahib herself, while we all clambered onto our
bikes and set off to school.

She was the one who 'ruled the roost' as she knew
everything there was to know about running a
successful household. She had worked for a Parsi pilot
(interestingly, he had been given the honour of flying
the plane which had scattered Jawaharlal Nehru's ashes
over the Himalayas) married to an Iranian former
student of New Era, as well as for other westerners for
over twenty-five years. Kripa was a fine cook and
produced some amazingly delicious Persian dishes as
well as good Indian food. She specialized in banana
fritters, which she'd cook for us at any time of the day
or night. We knew we were in good hands! Kripa also
liked to sew, so in her spare time (which she had quite
a lot of) she made us a very beautiful tablecloth
complete with scalloped edges. I had come across a
book on Rangavalli (Rangoli) art, and together, we
decided on some nice peacock designs taken from it
for her to sew.

It was about a twenty minute walk into the bazaar
and also to the main part of the school. We had bought

bikes in the bazaar for all of us from the local 'cycle-wallah.' Charlie, who was just turning seven years old, had a bike which had small wheels. The cycle-wallah had no tyres small enough to fit them so he cut two large tyres in half, making them a bit shorter by overlapping the ends and then gluing and stitching them back together again, before putting them onto the rims. When the wheels rotated, the bike bounced and made a sort of 'boo-doom' sound. The result was that poor Charlie occasionally ended up in the ditch which ran along each side of the rough road if he hit a pothole. This was not a good idea to do too often, as one was never quite sure what might be lurking down at the bottom!

Eventually, we moved to a smaller house on the main campus site which was far more convenient for us all and Kripa went back to Mumbai (Bombay) and into retirement. We were sad to lose her but her eyesight was failing and she could no longer walk to the bazaar, or carry the groceries. We settled down very happily in this little house, which was easier for school and much closer to the bazaar. We then went on a search for another ayah. We found a delightful young woman, called Usha who had two small boys. She was a very hard-working person and soon became part of the family. She didn't live in with us as Kripa had done, as she already lived up in the bazaar, but came to our house daily. She was very reliable. She eventually became a Baha'i as Charlie often talked to her about the Faith.

Where we lived, we were surrounded by the most amazing tropical sounds and the cicadas made continuous 'ksksks' noise from the trees in the heat of the day. Many monkeys lived around us and they were so funny to watch as they scampered around the grounds or picked the fleas out of each others' fur.

Green parrots flew in small flocks squawking around the place and the ubiquitous crows were ever present with their cawing.

With the relentless heat and dust that bore down on our heads continually for most of the year, the moment the monsoon arrived was a big event. Almost instantly, the brown earth turned into a most beautiful carpet of thick greenery. Flowers and shrubs of all different hues suddenly appeared as if by magic. The trees were decked in majestic foliage, so stunning in its variety that it took your breath away! It was truly a multi-coloured paradise. The parched earth drank her fill everywhere. The mountains continually spouted running streams and gushing falls.

It was during this season that there were many landslides. The roads could be blocked for days. The first week of the monsoon was heaven, but the downside of the monsoon season was the fact that it lasted for three whole months of non-stop deluge! Slowly, my spirits sagged, as day in and day out it would just continually pour down with rain, as if great buckets were being liberated of their contents on the tops of our heads from out of the sky. There were short moments of respite, when a somewhat watery sun would shine, and then we could all venture out tentatively with the fear of being totally drenched before we got home. At this time of the year, our shoes became covered in various shades of mould and our clothes started smelling badly. We felt permanently damp.

Whenever the opportunity arose, we went down to Pune on the local bus. This was a great bonus for us as we didn't often have much time to ourselves. During our travels, we saw many things. There were the usual beggars of all kinds and mahouts who accompanied their highly ornamented elephants, walking to and from the various temples. We saw little girls selling brightly coloured garlands of flowers. There would be people sitting on the ground sipping sweet tea or coffee and selling all kinds of things: from jewellery and clothes to painted statues. There were snake charmers and sellers of little bamboo flutes. Krishna's influence was to be seen everywhere. There was always some kind of interesting activity going on and the women walked by so gracefully in their bright-coloured saris, carrying brass water pots or beautifully woven baskets on their heads which were filled with different fruits or various household gadgets. Little herds of goats with tinkling bells around their necks trotted along the streets with their young goatherds. In the distance, the perpetual sounds of beautiful *bhajans* (devotional songs) could be heard mixed in with the less melodious soundtracks from popular Hindi movies.

Often, we came across a religious procession going along the roads to celebrate some festival or other for one of the many different gods. These processions were always very bright, raucous and crowded. Sometimes we would come across a marriage procession, where the bridegroom was to be seen riding along on a brightly decorated grey horse to the wedding.

Everybody was colourfully dressed and flower petals would be strewn all along the way. Monkeys could be seen chasing each other around and swinging from the trees even in the town. They sometimes attacked people, especially if they were carrying food. There was always the smell of incense mixed with spices, cow dung and urine pervading our senses wherever we went. Holy men were often seen doing *tapas* (austerities) of one kind or another. Others could be seen just standing around or walking along the roads to some far away pilgrimage site, alone, or with a crowd of others playing drums and a mixture of unusual looking wind instruments making an amazing noise, with the odd person dancing around. Animals roamed just about everywhere, especially cows, often with their horns brightly painted.

Outside peoples' homes there were often beautiful designs that had been made out of rice flour and different coloured powders. Some of the designs were extremely complex and included various sacred symbols. The local people did these designs as a means of protection for their homes. I noticed that ants liked to eat these edible powders. Nobody wanted a stream of ants marching into their homes. It was also considered an offering for the little creatures, as Indian people have a great respect for all of life. This art form was based on the Rangoli designs (the same that were used on the tablecloth that Kripa, our ayah, had made). These designs were created by using their fingers or a stick, using lines of dots. It was very clever. Sometimes white chalk was used, but I'm not so sure that the ants were quite so keen on that!

Everywhere one looked, there was evidence of a deeply spiritual and peaceful rhythm to the way people lived their lives. There was a gentle serenity that I noticed everywhere. I was deeply affected by the atmosphere of India. It seemed so much easier to devote oneself to the spiritual life than back in England. Although India is crowded, there somehow seems to be a sort of 'space' which is filled with an inexorable peace. I couldn't sense it so easily in the West. Spirituality was somehow entwined into every aspect of peoples' lives. I loved and welcomed its influence on me. It was amazing how happy people could be with so little material means and with such physical difficulties all around them.

The spiritual life of New Era School was the motivating, driving force for those who lived and worked there and many an early, chilly morning would find us going out with the rest of the school up onto the flat 'table land' of the surrounding smooth looking 'ghats' for dawn prayers. These early morning gatherings where we all shared prayers were very powerful and it was just heaven when the sun showed its first morning rays. Each moment became warmer and warmer as we all sat silently watching the sun rise, then everyone would troop back down the hill to school for breakfast. These ghats were extinct volcanoes and were hollow. They dominated the skyline, smooth in their formation. Not at all rugged like the Himalayas. Each one had a vast flat top, which is how they came to be called the 'table land', thereby giving Panchgani (five tables) its Marathi name.

At the school, many interesting events were put on for the benefit of the students. Indian classical dance classes were held regularly in the styles of Bharata Natyam and Kathakali, which originated from South India. The students put on a few dance dramas. There were a lot of music and theatre productions. I was invited to direct the musical *Oliver*. This was the main school play of the year and had a cast of sixty students. It was an amazing undertaking and one that I thoroughly enjoyed being involved with. Seeing these children of different races working together to create a performance was so heart-warming. Those who were in the show really began to develop more confidence in themselves. Some discovered they had a real talent for acting or singing and others discovered how to get along better with other members of the cast. It was great to see some individuals really flourish and begin to learn more about themselves where before they seemed to have not yet discovered an ability for doing very much. Many of the Indian staff got involved, exhibiting unexpected talents such as the art teacher creating the whole London skyline on a hessian sacking backdrop by means of spraying black paint from an old 'Flit' (fly spray) can.

There was also an active music department run by an enthusiastic Canadian, and the kids really enjoyed his classes. I began playing my flute again, having brought it to India, and the music teacher gave me a bit of extra tuition. It was the first time I had had any professional lessons. Being self- taught, I had learned some rather bad habits which I now had to try and unlearn! I soon became more confident and I started to play with others.

12 my chosen highway

EIGHT WEEKS OR SO after our arrival, I was invited to participate in a six-week musical trip, playing the flute, around South India. I had barely acclimatised to our new life, but this sounded like too great an opportunity to miss and I accepted. What an opportunity to see other parts of India. I was really excited.

We were called 'The Chosen Highway' and numbered seven in all: two other teachers, four students and myself. It was to be an unforgettable trip. We sang and played our way through Goa and down as far as the southernmost tip of the subcontinent. We visited many places, including Belgum, Mangalore, Bangalore, Cochin, Chennai (Madras) and Trivandrum, performing in many different venues. We saw many wonderful sights and made a few visits to temples and palaces along the way. Anyone who is familiar with the art of India will understand how I could fall in love with the highly decorative architecture and sculptures of the Hindu temples.

I was overwhelmed by the loving kindness and consideration from all the people we had the pleasure to meet. We stayed mainly in Bahá'í Centres wherever we went and when there was no actual Centre, we were welcomed into the homes of the local Bahá'ís, which was always a great pleasure. We performed in front of thousands of people giving performances wherever we went and teaching the message of the Bahá'í faith through the medium of song and music. The Indian students loved us. In some of the places we were mobbed by large crowds demanding our autographs. I began to understand what it might feel like to be a famous star!

For me this journey was much more than just a music trip. Several things occurred that helped me to get many things into perspective. I discovered that it was not very easy for us to be living in each other's laps for six weeks, day in day out. With all the exhausting travelling, tempers started to get frayed and it was good that we all took the time out in true Bahá'í spirit to discuss whatever the problem was. I learned a lot about human nature, but most of all I learned about myself. Travelling in India is not easy at the best of times and soon the first big test was awaiting me . . .

We arrived at our destination in the middle of an absolutely sweltering Indian afternoon. We had been travelling for two long days on a variety of trains and local buses virtually non-stop, over a huge distance, before arriving exhausted and wet through with perspiration at the local Bahá'í Centre to find only a cleaner there. We were hungry and thirsty and had not been able to wash properly either during the journey. We were told there was no water and that it was only available for an hour in the morning. I was unprepared for this. The other staff members and students on this trip were well seasoned travellers, having lived and travelled around India for several years, so they were coping a lot better than I was.

This Bahá'í Centre was nowhere near the centre of the town, and the nearest café or access to any food was a long, hot ride away by autorickshaw. What were we to do? We all sat down together somewhat dejected until eventually one of the local Bahá'ís turned up.

I went in search of the loo. To my horror, I discovered a very small, dark room, with a tap in the wall, a couple of plastic buckets and a small metal jug. Not a drop of water was to be seen. This was the last straw! I couldn't bear it and I wept unconsolably for ages crouched in this spot.

I thought to myself, 'How on earth am I going to last out the trip?' Here I was, a week's journey away from Panchgani and with another five weeks ahead of me. I felt I had definitely made the wrong decision to go on this trip so soon after arriving in India. What a stupid fool I was. My sense of adventure had really got the better of me this time. How would I ever cope? Could I continue? Would I make it? India was presenting me with so many tests . . .

Slowly, I calmed down, but still feeling really sorry for myself. I recognised that I was being tested. There was no question of my turning back now. I knew that it would be impossible anyway. As I contemplated my next move, a stillness began to seep into my angry mind and a lightness of spirit slowly descended on me. I felt as if I was somehow being helped from some deep source. A profound peace was very definitely beginning to fill my mind. Calmness soothed my brow. I had squeezed out all the tears that remained in me. I stood up and made a decision. I was not going to allow myself to fall victim to any more negative thoughts. This kind of thinking was so destructive and totally unhelpful. This trip was the opportunity of a lifetime and I was not going to mess it up now. Slowly, I started to feel better and stronger. I wiped my face, collected myself and joined the others.

In the meantime, the miracle had happened. Food had appeared from somewhere and tea was on its way. Wow, things were definitely beginning to look up. All I needed to do was learn to trust more. It seemed so simple yet . . . Things usually have a habit of turning out okay if only we allow it to happen. From then on, it seemed to get a little easier. Why? Was it my mind? Was I being helped somehow? I began to discover new ways of tapping into those resources which lay deep within me. I knew that this was what I really needed now in order to cope with whatever difficult situations came my way, but first I had to let go of all my preconceived ideas and expectations...

I started to dream a lot during this trip. The dreams were helpful in their content and I began to feel that I was being guided and blessed. One dream was of Ruhhiyih Khanum appearing, smiling in a kindly sort of way. I started to feel different about myself. I felt empowered and supported and somehow knew that things would be easier for me as the trip continued. These dreams, which seemed more like visionary teachings were to continue at a very regular rate, right through the rest of the trip. This journey was a major turning point for me in my life.

I had been able to literally 'change my mind' into a much more positive state of being. Now, I began to see that the rest of the trip could be a big adventure and I accepted whatever came my way. Eventually, we arrived at a Bahá'í Centre in another large town. Most of the communities we visited along the way had a few Persians or other 'pioneers', as they were called, living there who had come from other parts of the world. It was a pleasant surprise to find that this particular Bahá'í community were all Indian except for two beautiful Persian sisters. Everyone was truly delightful and welcomed us in. They couldn't do enough to make us feel at home. I was so touched by their love. Indian hospitality really comes from the heart.

During our stay, the community got together for the Commemoration of the Martyrdom of the Bab, everybody was invited to say some prayers. The Bab was the forerunner of Bahá'u'llah and he said that someone greater than himself would come to teach humanity. The Bab's ministry lasted only six years. He was martyred as a young man in the square of Tabriz, Persia in 1850. For this event, I was asked to read the 'Tablet of Visitation'. We were all sitting round the room in a large circle. The men one side and the women the other. When I had finished reading this Tablet, in the silent and still moment that followed, a most extraordinary event began to unfold . . .

I find myself standing, surrounded by a very large crowd. Loud noises fill the air. The crowd is extremely agitated and the atmosphere is emotionally highly charged. There is crashing and shouting all around me. Suddenly, dust and smoke fills the area. It is hot and I am being jostled about in a tumultuous, hostile crowd. The noise is amazingly intense and the crowd is massive and oppressive. I see the whole square and the buildings which surround it. I look at Godfrey, who happens to be standing on my right with our two sons at his side. Again I look ahead and see before me the Bab suspended and hanging with another young man, quite near to a building, waiting to be shot. What . . . I can't believe it! What is going on? A thought runs through my head . . . It seems I have to choose . . . My family, or the Bab, the path of spirit?

Then the vision disappeared. Was this a past life flashback? . . . But Bahá'ís don't believe in reincarnation . . . which was something that I found hard to accept, because I had always believed in having past lives and possibly we would also have future ones . . . Could it be that all our lives occur simultaneously? In which case, arguments for or against reincarnation would be waste of time!

I was not fully conscious for the next two days. It seems that the two young Persian sisters had taken it upon themselves to look after me. I have no recollection of how I ate or where I slept. I was completely in a trance. Two days later, I found myself returning to a somewhat more normal state. From that moment on, I felt very close to the message of the Bab. Later, I was to read an interesting book that described what had happened on that fateful day and found that my experience completely corroborated the events that had been recorded by eye witnesses in Tabriz.

Several other events happened to me along the way. They were strong messages which helped me on my spiritual journey. I became calmer and more relaxed. Things seemed easier. Everyone was kind. Along the way, I met many interesting people such as Gopi, a beautiful Bahá'i Carnatic singer. He was living in one of the local Bahá'i centres for a while and practised regularly every morning and evening along with another singer who may have been one of his students. I loved listening to his rich and melodious voice which was enchanting. I asked him if he would teach me something. He was happy that I was interested and agreed, but I would have to get up early every morning ready to start at six a.m. So, early the next day I was up and learning to sing the Carnatic scale. I found it was quite easy to pick up and I was inspired. For the next five mornings I practiced with him and again at eleven each night. As I mastered the scale, he started teaching me some simple prayers to chant. At the end of my stay he kindly made a cassette tape for me so that I could continue my practice. Any spare moments I had to myself, I spent practicing the songs and scales.

Finally, it was the end of the six weeks and time to return to Panchgani. The trip had been a testing but exciting one. Now I was ready to return to my husband and children, feeling totally spiritually renewed.

13 family values

THE SCHOOL WAS very privileged to have two very fine Indian classical dancers, a husband and wife team called the Gopalakrishnans. Ever since seeing some Indian classical dances on the television as a youngster, I had wanted to learn it. Now was my chance. So, having recovered from my trip around South India I asked Smt. Gopalakrishnan if she would take me on as one of her students. She agreed and I began my studies in Bharata Natyam under her ever watchful eye. (Bharata Natyam is the famous temple dance form from South India).

Smt. Gopalakrishnan was a wonderful teacher and inspired me greatly. She had been a famous Indian classical dancer in her time and had travelled and performed all over the world, as had her husband who had been a very famous Kathakali dancer and choreographer. He had been the first choreographer for the Tamil screen. He now taught many folk dances and dance dramas in the school. Through this beautiful dance form, I was introduced to the stories from the Mahabharata and the Ramayana, the ancient legends of Hinduism. I also learned several of the folk dances from around the different states of India and as a result of my studies, I began to understand more about Hinduism. I learnt about how the gods represented the different aspects of Brahman (God). It was all so fascinating.

Through my dance teacher, I had the opportunity to study the sitar under the tutelage of Sri Kelkarji, a talented musician who had played violin in the orchestra of Uday Shankar, the elder brother of Ravi Shankar, the famous sitarist. Sri Kelkarji was also a very talented sitarist in his own right, as well as being an excellent teacher. He lived in a most beautiful and ancient house, formerly part of Shivaji's stables, in the pilgrimage town of Wai, an hour's run down the ghats. Once a week, I eagerly took my sitar for a bumpy taxi ride to my lesson. Sri Kelkarji taught me how to get in touch with that underlying magic, which is at the heart of all Indian classical music. Playing the sitar took me to that silent, eternal place, where I learned how I could become 'one' with the instrument. The whole of life seemed to become reflected in its sweet, harmonious tones as I played and 'listened' with my whole body. It was ecstatic. Learning about the music also helped me to perform better as a dancer. The music and dance nourished my soul. I had had the best teachers that India could possibly offer, enabling me to touch that sublime pinnacle of divine expression which comes from the heart.

There were many ways in which as a family we all found creative expression in our lives in this little corner of India. The boys were exploring all kinds of things and learning new skills. Charlie was particularly happy here. He had found a teacher in the school who was on his wavelength and helped him with his school work. She was a beautiful and very patient American lady who was married to an Indian who taught maths in the school. She found out that Charlie was dyslexic. As soon as this was discovered, a whole programme was created especially for him. As a result, he made tremendous progress. We were delighted to see him so happy. Both the boys made many new friends who came from different parts of the world.

One day there was a great hullabaloo going on outside and we wondered if a tribe of monkeys had descended onto the corrugated roof of the house. So we rushed out and saw that it was Charlie with five other little friends having a great old time. A Somali, American, Canadian, and two Indian boys made up the party. It was a sight to behold!

Amongst the many visitors who came to the school was a man who was a Bahá'í Counsellor and a friend of the school. He had a bad heart, so he had to be very careful whenever he came up to Panchgani because of the altitude. He was one of the most illuminating people I was ever to have the privilege to meet and I had some wonderfully inspiring discussions with him on the few occasions he was with us.

At the same time, I made friends with a young American woman who was the daughter of a Rabbi. It was interesting that we had similar backgrounds, especially when we found out that we both independently had a mutual friend in Counsellor Nagaratnam. She had given him some reflexology which had greatly helped him. So it wasn't surprising, that one night should find the three of us in his room, spending time together . . .

The room was a real rose garden of peace with the fragrances of pure devotion and love filling all of our hearts. In the loving presence of Counsellor Nagaratnam, we were illuminated as we spoke only of the nectar of immortality. We both so loved this wonderful, inspired man who could only love from the heart.

One day, I was invited to run a series of courses on 'Family Life' for women who came from all over India to the Bahá'í Academy, which was based in Panchgani. This was a great opportunity for me to study the Bahá'í writings on this particular aspect. These were very beautiful teachings that showed us how to communicate better with each other and, at the same time, develop more consideration for each family member so that we could become a stronger, more loving unit. They taught me that the first community is the family and this was the place where we could really start demonstrating our love for each other. We needed to learn wisdom and develop more patience; to 'listen' more to the needs of each other and look for ways of helping one another out whenever it was necessary. If we could really manifest this level of love and patience within the family, then it would be possible to create a very beautiful community around us. Our villages, towns, countries and even the whole world could begin to live in peace together. It was a very powerful teaching. I really believed that if we could manage to have a peaceful and happy family unit to start with, then it would be possible to bring about actual world peace. I was greatly excited about that possibility.

The women on this course welcomed discussion on how to create more loving homes for their families. During the teaching of this course, I started to see what was beginning to happen within my own family. Our children were involved in the many activities of the school and I didn't see much of them. They were either in class or playing with their friends. Sometimes they stayed in the dormitories if we had to go 'out of station' to visit outlying villages or down to Pune. A lot of villagers had become Bahá'ís and we went and visited them at fairly regular intervals, teaching them the various aspects of the faith. Godfrey was very busy running the senior school and he was also secretary of the Local Spiritual Assembly. This was the administrative body that looked after the very large local community of Bahá'ís in Panchgani. We didn't

see much of each other. I began to feel somewhat bereft
. . . We were in danger of disintegrating as a family
unit. We needed to spend more time together if it was
to be resolved. Godfrey and I talked about it and we
both recognised the need for some sort of change in
our programme so that we could have some more time
together. This was not as easy as we hoped. Other
families also found it hard to find time to be together.

Was I being selfish to question this? I asked myself.
Yes, I suppose I was, but I needed my husband's
companionship and support and yes, I wanted to spend
time with my children. Then I thought that this kind
of selfishness was a good thing, as everybody would
benefit from it. This was what the course on Family
Life was all about. Unfortunately, there wasn't much
any of us could do about it the way things were, so
eventually we decided that the best thing to do was to
return to England. The circumstances in India were
changing, and this influenced our decision to return.
The political situation in India had become difficult after
the assassination of Indira Gandhi and for the first time
since independence, British citizens were now required
to have work visas. This would make things difficult
for us. Godfrey left first so that he could prepare for
the work he had been offered back in Coventry.

Meanwhile, I went on a school trip to Kulu and
Manali which was as close to Kashmir as the growing
political crisis in that region would allow me to get.
The area was stunningly beautiful and gave me a good
idea of the Kashmiri landscape as well as of its flora
and fauna. On the way up the mountain I came within
a hair's breadth of ending my life when the driver
started to fall asleep at the wheel of our coach.
Fortunately, I was sitting near the front and could see
that although the road was bending ahead of us to the
right, the driver was steering us straight ahead! I

shouted to get his attention and for the rest of the trip the two tour guides stood behind him to ensure that he kept awake.

This trip provided a fitting climax to the two years I had spent in India with memories that would stay with me until my return.

moving on

"...I stand
On this
Lonely shore
A seeker
Seeking
The
Beloved One..."

(Poems from My Heart,
'In Memory of a Fellow Lover of the Light')

14 a short prelude

HAVING LEFT Nicolas in India to complete his school year as a boarder, I flew back with Charles to join Godfrey in the small cottage we owned just outside Rugby in Warwickshire. The readjustment to western living proved difficult for all of us. Godfrey struggled back to comprehensive school teaching where the social problems seemed to have increased greatly during the two years we had been away. Charles missed his friends and the support of staff at New Era High School and found it difficult to lose the unique accent he had acquired there. My first shopping expedition in Rugby ended literally in tears, as Godfrey rescued me from the complexities of having to weigh out fruit and vegetables on scales (which produced a price tag ready for the check-out) when for two years I had simply bargained in the local bazaar. It was all too much!

We had some good Persian friends in Rugby and neighbouring Warwick, including Mandana who had lived with us before going to India. Godfrey was elected chairman of the local Bahá'ís but we found it all rather dull after Panchgani. Nevertheless, we were lucky to have a ready-made circle of friends including a Persian couple nearby who had rented our house whilst we were in India. I decided to try and overcome the inevitable gain in weight which returning to a western diet entailed. These friends lived about a mile away and so, full of good intentions, I changed into running clothes and set off on a daily jog to their house. Persians are well known for their hospitality and when I arrived, slightly out of breath, my hostess always offered me coffee and a rather large slice of her delicious home-made cake. After a couple of weeks of this regime, I tired of trying to get fit and took out the bicycle instead. It was quicker. Within no time at all, the weight had returned but the cake was more more delicious than ever . . .

One of the local Bahá'ís we had known before moving to India was an accomplished concert pianist and we were invited by a friend to attend a concert he was giving in Coventry Cathedral. He played brilliantly and afterwards he introduced us to another musician who had been a master at Rugby School for many years. John Graves proved to be a wonderful friend and accompanist, inspiring me to pursue my study of the flute. He was quite elderly, but he had infinite patience, ability and a lifetime of teaching experience. The few months we spent in Rugby turned out to be a real musical feast. John would come round regularly to our home and help me through my pieces for the flute. It was a great encouragement to find someone who lived and breathed music as he did and we remained in close contact after we moved that summer to Worcester, until his death a few years later.

GODFREY HAD found himself a far more rewarding teaching post in Worcester in an independent day school where we also were able to send Nicolas. We found a primary school for Charles with a teacher who was sympathetic to his special needs. We gradually began to settle down to a new rhythm of life.

Once again, providence appeared in the form of a musical neighbour, Joy who helped me get to grips with music theory which I needed if I was to be successful in getting into music college. She also played the bassoon in a local orchestra and suggested that I might like to join it.

How could I possibly play in an orchestra with so little experience as a flautist? I wondered. I soon discovered how when Joy took me to the first rehearsal which could only be described as unique. The orchestra was run by an indomitable lady who somehow managed to hold everything together, which was quite a challenge given that the average age was at least seventy and that the level of musicianship was uneven to say the least. Still, it was great fun, I learned a lot and our audiences even paid to come and listen to us!

So having passed my Grade Five theory examination, I embarked on a two year music diploma course to continue studying the flute. Normally, one would have to study the piano as a second instrument but the piano teacher in the college, an international concert pianist, was also a harpist and he offered to teach me harp. I was thrilled to have this opportunity and so I took up the harp. I liked the way he taught and I flourished under his expert guidance. Even if I just ran my fingers across the harp, it sounded wonderful. This time in my life was to be a period of self-exploration through working in the creative arts.

I started giving some private classes in Bharata Natyam dance at home in our lounge and some members of the Krishna Consciousness Movement started coming along to them. I enjoyed teaching these people as they were so enthusiastic about India and its culture. We often joined them for bhajans and kirtans chanting devotional songs of Lord Krishna. I eventually set up some general dance classes in the Old Quilt Factory, which had been turned into an Arts Centre, in the centre of Worcester.

The Arts Centre promoted many different activities one of which was a large community play with some two thousand people in it. I was one of three assistant directors who helped the main director to run the rehearsals. People came from all walks of life and the cast included a couple of professional actors. It was a lot of fun, working with so many different kinds of people of all ages.

Once a week, I took myself to a Kathak dance class in Birmingham, which was being run by Nahid Siddiqui, a famous performer. I loved these classes. One day, I had had such a good class that I spent all my time driving home thinking about it. I was so absorbed in my thoughts that I missed the two different exits off the M5 motorway to Worcester and found myself on the way to Tewkesbury! Not having any money on me at the time and with virtually no petrol left in the tank, I began to panic. Eventually, I saw an exit and I was able to turn around and get home just before completely running out of petrol! Wow, how our minds play tricks on us.

It was good to be together again as a family but we still often thought of India. In particular, I missed the friends we had made as well as those 'little' things which often passed unnoticed during an average day over there but which now took on greater significance, like looking out of the windows and seeing the sun shining most of the time and the frequent sounds of Indian music wafting over the air waves in the distance as we went about our business.

After a couple of years of being in the UK, an opportunity to go back to India came our way. A girls' international school in the Himalayas wanted a Principal. There were not very many advertisements for teaching jobs in India so when one came along we thought long and hard about it. Funnily enough, Godfrey had been offered this post a year previously but we then had felt it was too soon for us to go back. Now we all agreed as a family that it was time to go for it.

So, in July1986 we packed our bags, sold the house and furniture and off we all went to settle in the really beautiful hill-station of Mussoorie, north of Delhi in Uttar Pradesh. This time, we knew so much more about life in India that we decided to take our little miniature daschund, Kizzy with us.

SHORTLY AFTER arriving in Delhi, we were met and taken by car all the way up to Mussoorie. It was a good seven hour trip and we broke down along the way. There we sat, in the baking heat of the day, soon rescued by a man passing by on a bicycle who just happened to be a car mechanic. India is amazing. It was good to be back again.

When we finally approached Mussoorie, it was already dark and as we looked up into what we thought was the night sky, we were surprised to see a long line of twinkling lights shimmering high above us. The sight just took our breath away. It was awesome! We were on the edge of our seats with excitement. We had finally arrived.

The next task was to find schools for the boys. Nicolas went to Woodstock, an American international school. Charlie, we felt, would have a better chance if we sent him to a different school without the pressures from his elder brother. So he went to Guru Nanak School where there were already quite a lot of westerners. But after only three days, it was obvious that he was not happy, so we withdrew him and sent him to Woodstock too. They both became boarders as there were frequent landslides between us and their school and the roads could remain blocked for days on end. Nicolas liked his teacher. Charlie struggled as

101

nobody in the school seemed to understand his dyslexia. After a few months, he came and lived with us in our school. The good news was that Myrna, his old teacher from Panchgani days, and her husband had come and joined Godfrey's staff in Mussoorie, and she volunteered to carry on teaching him. This turned out to be a great arrangement and he was happy.

Our school nestled into the side of the Himalayan foothills some seven thousand feet up. We were surrounded by the most spectacular views of the huge, snow clad Himalayan peaks rising in layers into the distance. Dawn and dusk were the most spectacular times of day and lit up the snows like a fairytale painting. There was a pretty little white Hindu temple perched on the top of a small hill just below us which looked as if it was magically suspended in space when the clouds floated by.

Just above the school there was a community of Tibetans living in an area known as 'Happy Valley'. Happy Valley is where the Dalai Lama first came, when he arrived in exile from Tibet. The Tibetan school was run by the Dalai Lama's niece. She was a very lovely lady who often invited us to various events at her school. We saw many learned Tibetan lamas who occasionally visited Happy Valley from the Buddhist monasteries in and around India and sometimes we saw some of the Buddhist monks gather together at a crossroads just below the Library Bazaar. They were a very colourful sight and we were quite surprised on several occasions to see a western Buddhist monk amongst them as he was so tall and white against the small, swarthy Tibetans.

The Tibetans in Happy Valley continued to live very much in their traditional way. They had kept their beautiful clothes, arts and language. They had also brought their own little dogs all the way from Tibet. The Tibetan dogs are short with long hair and when I walked Kizzy up the hill, the Tibetans were intrigued by her long sausage-like body and short fur. In fact, she was unlike anything they had ever seen before. They just stared and stared at her with broad grins on their faces.

The Tibetans are a warm and welcoming people who have suffered a great deal and who have successfully created a new home for themselves in India, bringing with them their rich heritage and spirituality. It is interesting how India manages to hold and absorb into itself so many different kinds of people and their cultures.

I learned something about the Buddhist way of life as we had some Tibetans working in the school with whom we became friendly. These wonderful people found happiness through simple living. I was struck by how they could be so content with the little that they had. Life in Happy Valley was simple. I too desired that element of simplicity in my own life. Here in India I had touched the earth where Sages had walked for millennia. How very fortunate I was to have an opportunity to be in this most sacred of places.

One day, whilst we were in the bazaar, we came across an interesting bookshop that had books in English as well as the Indian languages. We went in and had a look around. A book called "Living With The Himalayan Masters" by Swami Rama, caught my eye so I purchased it. It was about the life of Swami Rama, who from a very early age, had been raised in the mountain caves of the various different sages. I could not stop reading it over and over and was so impressed with this swami.

Eventually, my parents came over to visit us for a couple of weeks and I showed this book to them. They were really interested in it and they said that Swami Rama was the guru of Usharbudh Arya who had stayed with us on quite a few occasions in Gloucestershire all those years ago. When they returned home, they contacted Usharhudh Arya after having taken down the details from this book, and eventually went and visited Swami Rama in America and became initiates of the Himalayan Tradition.

Ironically, I was completely unaware at the time that Usharhbudh Arya was actually living in Dehra Dun with all his family, just an hour's run down the hill from Mussoorie. He and his wife ran a leper colony there, with a school for the children of lepers. Usharbudh and his wife also helped at the hospital which Swami Rama of the Himalayas had set up. If I had known, I could have reconnected with this friend of thirty odd years before, but that was not to happen until quite some time later. How strange life is. It seems that what is meant to happen, happens when it is meant to and what is not meant to happen, never will happen.

17 the cosmic dance

ON ONE OF our trips down to Delhi, we discovered that the national school of Kathak dance, Kathak Kendra was situated not far from where we normally stayed when visiting Delhi. I was keen to continue my study of dance and had quite a lot of free time on my hands during the school week so I decided to see if I could go and study there.

Once, we had been to see Pandit Sri Durga Lal, a famous dancer, giving an amazing performance in Dehra Dun. He was teaching at the Kendra and so I decided to ask whether he would take me on as his student. He agreed. I did a puja and made an offering for him in the traditional Indian manner before being accepted. I became a student of Indian dance again. There are several different styles (gharanas), of Kathak dance and with Sri Durga Lalji, I studied the Jaipur Gharana style of Kathak. This is a very energetic form of Kathak dance and very fast. Physically, it was a challenge, but I loved the classes. I was introduced to Sri Birju Maharaj, a world famous Kathak dancer who also taught at the school when he wasn't on tour, which, unfortunately, was a lot of the time. He taught the Lucknow Gharana which was a much softer form that appealed to me. I spent some time talking with him about the ballet and danced for him. He agreed to my joining his class too.

The heat was almost unbearable—often around 46 degrees centigrade and we danced in large rooms whose only form of ventilation was a couple of big fans built into the ceiling. These fans only worked for the first half hour of the day, then they cut right out. At one point, I became so dehydrated that I became virtually unconscious and fell sick for three days. Our driver had introduced us to a delightful couple on one of our trips down to Delhi and over time, we had become good friends, especially now I was able to see them more frequently. Fortunately, they lived quite close to the Kendra and I was able to get the chokhidar (guard) to go and get them to come to the rescue. They took me to their place in a rickshaw and looked after me, not that I was much aware of it. Under their careful ministrations, I recovered fairly quickly. Godfrey knew nothing about it as our friends could not get hold of him on the telephone. Telephoning in those days was a bit of a 'hit and miss' affair.

At the Kendra, I made friends with a young American contemporary dancer, Shalini, who had had a similar dance background to mine. She was a vegetarian like me and had an exuberant nature which belied an inner calm. She turned out to be a disciple of Chökyal Namkhai Norbu, who was a Tibetan Lama living in Italy. Having come into contact with Tibetans up in Happy Valley already, I was interested to know more about their beliefs and practices. Shalini explained to me that this Lama gave the Buddhist teachings on non-duality or the 'Primordial' as she referred to it. These teachings are known as Dzogchen and are the very high teachings of the Nyingmapa school, the oldest tradition of Tibetan Buddhism. Shalini said that she had spent three days on a retreat in a cave with this Lama. I was intrigued to know more. She told me how powerful the teachings were and how they could change one's life. One evening she played me a tape of this teacher chanting in a very deep, resonant voice. It profoundly affected me. The sound was like a shock wave to my consciousness. Yes, I thought, this could change my life. Later, she gave me an inspiring book written by Namkhai Norbu, called 'The Crystal and the Way of Light'. I found it a remarkable book which contained extraordinary teachings.

This 'natural state' that this Master referred to, seemed to be so accessible, yet, at the same time, it was a very difficult concept to take on board. I 'knew' that this was the sort of spiritual knowledge that I really wanted to have. The secret was that we have to get beyond 'techniques' and become one with the 'Primordial'. The 'Primordial', being our 'natural' state, or 'original state'. The state beyond the mind. No other spiritual teachings that I had explored had dealt with this aspect, although I had had many experiences in my life that showed me that there was much more to existence than met the eye . . .

The Dzogchen teachings reminded me of a conversation I had had as a small child with my old friend, with the beard. He had brought a bag of chocolates with him and the two of us had gone out for a short walk . . .

He said, 'My dearest one, what is on your mind?' He knew I always had lots of questions to ask him.

I hesitated for a few moments to gather my thoughts, then I said, 'The other day, some people came to visit us and they were talking about... the "natural state" or "awakened state" and I wanted to know what they were talking about. It was all very mysterious, and when I asked them what they meant, they said that I was far too young to worry about such things and anyway I would find it boring because I wouldn't understand . . . so I thought I would ask you. Do you know what they could have been talking about? I heard one of them saying that we can only discover this awakened state gradually. Another believed that it happened instantly. I am really interested and I do want to know! Can you tell me anything about this and what it all means?'

'Umm,' he said, 'that is a very deep question from one so young . . . ' and he gave me a loving, searching, look. 'The "awakened state" is where suddenly we see very clearly into the meaning of . . . **all** things. This can also be called the "natural state".'

I interrupted, 'Like seeing the inside of the outside, and the outside of the inside?' remembering something he had once said . . .

He smiled, with his loving, twinkly eyes, 'Yes, it is just like that. An "awakening" is when one really and truly **"knows"** with the whole of one's being, that the inside and the outside, are really one and the same thing. Where one has a glimpse of God or a glimpse into . . . *Who* you truly are, which is absolutely what you **naturally** are. Yes. This "natural state" is the state of who, how and what, we actually are, **before** we have superimposed a false identity onto ourselves. What I mean by "superimposed" is that we have created a personality or an image of ourselves, and given it a name and a form that everybody else can also relate to, then we get into the bad habit of assuming that that is who we really are.'

'Okay, but what is God?'

He answered that God actually **was** that 'natural state', the 'awakened state'. God was absolutely everything . . . and that also included all of us too. Sometimes people try to personalise God, which is fine as far as it goes, but truly, God was pure consciousness or vibration.

God was not separate from us at all. In fact we were all an intrinsic part of God. We are that pure consciousness. What an amazing thought.

Then I said, 'The awakened state that these people were talking about is like having a *glimpse* all the time, like a . . . continuous glimpse – one that never went away?'

He laughed and said, 'yes, indeed, my dearest. Just like a continuous glimpse, happening all the time!'

'That must be an amazing state to be in, and all the time. I wish I could experience that,' I sighed.

Then my old friend, turned to me and with a very serious manner, he said, 'Of course you can experience it.'

'Have you experienced it?'

His response was, 'All the time I experience it.'

'All the time?' I said, surprised.

'Yes, a continuous glimpse happening all the time!'

Wow! Was this the reason why I loved this man so much? What was it about him that really attracted my attention? He seemed to me to have all the qualities of a truly perfect person. He was loving, wise, caring, and, boy, could he listen. He was generous with his time with me and he knew so much . . .

Whenever I was with him, a feeling of calm would always envelop me. Amazing . . .

A silence and stillness overcame me as I was thinking about what he had just said.

Then, he interrupted my thoughts . . . 'This **is** our natural state. It is nothing new. You are already in the "natural state", but you think that you have to go somewhere and search for it, but it is who you are. Where can you go to find it when it is in you already?

'Listen very carefully and I will explain how you can come to know it.

'First, there is the gradual process of becoming a better person. That is, by being honest and trustworthy in our behaviour towards others. Speaking the truth at all times. When you are kind or generous or being helpful and considerate to another person or perhaps helping or being kind to some animal **just for the sake of it** and not because you want something back in return. This is what I would say is a process of **"cleaning out the vessel"**. This "vessel" is your body and mind, and you can turn it into a pure, clean and beautiful place. A place where pure truth would like to stay. This is not what I would call *awakening* but rather a preparation that will help you to become open and receptive and more able to recognize the truth of it. This could be considered the *gradual* bit. And secondly, the *awakened* state, I would say, is recognizing and really **knowing** by actually experiencing our own selves as being that *pure consciousness*. This *consciousness* is always present, always and for ever, and it is known instantly. This can also be called the "natural" state if you like. It is all things and is absolutely everywhere.

'It is the inside of the outside as well as being the outside of the inside, like I said before and you are that pure consciousness already. It is only when you tune in to your own being-ness that you *wake up* into that state of pure consciousness. Pure awareness itself.

'This is an invitation . . . awakening is about living and being *present* in the NOW. Right now, not five minutes ago, nor in five minutes' time. I repeat, you are already that pure consciousness which comes before anything that you **think you are!**'

The Dzogchen teachings seemed to be similar to what my old friend had been talking about. These are some of the thoughts that were going round and round my head . . .

- The 'natural state' is our true state. Was this something other than our normal conscious awareness? Speaking words of 'definition' confuses my understanding of the real nature of things.

'Reality is' . . . Umm . . .

There is no way of explanation . . . No words can I find, that really explain the ultimate truth or reality. So, does the mind really have anything to do with it?

Does the mind have to 'vacate' itself in order for the 'revelation' to come in? No mind?

Silence gives us the reward we seek . . .

Where silence is, all answers are to be found . . .

Is it possible to understand the true meaning of Love, Truth or Compassion?

We are caught up in the shadow . . . the shadow-play of thoughts and words. The words **are** the shadow! The thought that 'all things are me' is the shadow that confuses me. Thoughts just confuse me!

Once we understand that we don't need words, then we are free . . . . FREE!

We have restricted and limited ourselves and everything to our own small ego's perspective.

We are the underlying substratum of all that is. We have superimposed everything else (world) onto the substratum. That is an amazing fact!

That this is God. If this is so, then we all must be God or at the very least, aspects of God. This must be God-Consciousness . . . and if one doesn't believe in God, is it still valid? So 'Source' or 'Divinity' would be the same thing? Definitely.

We are already **that** . . . I am there already . . . ? Ummm!

The course at Kathak Kendra was well planned and rigorous but there was also time for personal space and reflection and I continued to think very deeply about these thoughts and shared them with Shalini. Every morning at six o'clock, before my dance class, I went to a yoga session run by an ex-dancer who came and taught the students in one of the large rooms at the Kendra. One particular morning, towards the end of the class, I experienced an interesting moment. Whilst sitting quietly on the floor, with my body feeling totally relaxed, I just happened to glance up to see the teacher writing something in Sanskrit on the blackboard. To my surprise, I found that I could actually read and understand it. I just 'knew' it was a quotation from the Vedas. So I began writing it down. I was amazed. How was it possible for me to read it, let alone understand it? I had never studied Sanskrit—certainly not in this lifetime. As I got up to leave, I mentioned to her what had just happened. She was very excited and wanted to talk some more, but we had no time, as the next lot of students were already arriving for their class . . .

This experience showed me clearly, that it is definitely possible to tap into all knowledge that is in the whole universe, if only we knew how to do it. A few hours later my mind became clouded again and I lost the ability to read what I had written down let alone understand it! I knew that I had been given another glimpse of that underlying reality. That substratum, that I had had a sense of, as a small child. This was what my old bearded friend had been telling me about all those years ago. This experience was truly a gift from the divine. I realised that we actually have to *experience* this pure consciousness in order to really know it. It was not enough just to have an intellectual understanding of it. In my day-to-day life, I found that some of my questions were being answered.

In between my Kathak classes, I enrolled nearby, in some classical singing classes and just as I was enquiring about some sitar lessons, an Indian gentleman (Sri Myadhar Raut) approached me and said I should join his Odissi dance classes. So I abandoned the sitar lessons and began learning Odissi dance instead, with this lovely gentleman. Odissi is the main dance form from the state of Orissa and it was a great opportunity to study another form of dance learning enough to be able to perform a Mangala Charan.

At the Kendra, those of us who lived in the hostel would be treated from time to time with a visit from Birju Maharaj who brought out his harmonium and sat with us in the courtyard and sang devotional music. These impromptu performances were a great pleasure and a precious gift which transported me beyond time and space. He was a very fine artist.

Often, Man Mohan, our driver from school would be in Delhi having brought people down, and he would drop by Kathak Kendra to see if I would like a ride back up to Mussoorie. This was a great arrangement as he always had a knack of appearing when I didn't have much to do. I was keen to go back up into the cool of the mountains for a few days and see Godfrey again. Delhi was so hot.

After a couple of years of living in this beautiful paradise, we had to make some family decisions once again, partly because of the needs of our children. Nicolas, decided that he wanted to leave school now that he was nearly seventeen. If he left, he would not be able to stay in India unless he remained a student, so he would have to return to the UK. He was adamant that he wanted to leave. We made some enquiries and I flew back with him and arranged for him to stay with some old friends in Worcester as a paying guest. He then enrolled on a youth training scheme where he could get work experience and at the same time, earn some money. It was hard leaving him alone in England while I flew back to India, but at least I could rest in the knowledge that he was amongst friends who would keep an eye on him. Charlie, now twelve years old was in need of some serious specialist education. He had had some great help through Myrna but he needed more. So we planned our return to England. We had enjoyed the second Indian experience, but it was obvious that we could not remain there as things were.

Godfrey went to England for a short visit to see what he could find job-wise. I continued with my studies in Indian Classical dance at the Kendra in Delhi and Charlie came and stayed with me in the Kendra hostel. During the classes, Charlie sat on the side with the musicians and fell in love with the sounds of the tablas. He loved the rhythms and he became friends with the tabla players.

During my time in Delhi, I had joined a group of international dancers who went around giving performances in some of the five-star hotels. We had a performance coming up at a private party in one of these hotels and Charlie came along to the rehearsals. He loved to dance and was invited to perform some of his break-dancing which he was brilliant at doing. He was very good at spinning around on a finger or an elbow, or swinging on his back then leaping back up onto his feet. In the five-minute slot that he was given, he stole the show!

Just before Godfrey was due back to India, we all celebrated the Diwali festival of Lights. This we did with Sri Mayadhar Raut, his wife and some of the other Odissi students. We decorated the balcony outside the studio with candles. It was very beautiful. At the end of the evening, Man Mohan, our driver, came and picked us both up to go and collect Godfrey from the airport. Godfrey returned having fixed himself up with a·temporary, two term teaching job in Essex. This would tide us over until we found something more permanent.

Just before returning to the UK, Godfrey and Charlie went for a final holiday to Calangute in Goa whilst I finished my course at the Kathak Kendra. At the end of it, I travelled by train with Ashok, the son of my friends who lived just around the corner from the Kendra. He was going to sell sandwiches on the beach in Goa. The decent buses had all left Pune and what was left was an old, rickety Maharashtra State Transport bus with only six passengers aboard who were prepared to risk the journey. This last bit entailed an overnight ride and it turned out to be a very bumpy one as my seat was not attached to its frame! At one point, Ashok went to ask the driver to go more slowly, but to his surprise, he saw two drivers: one sitting on the lap of the other and both driving at the same time. One was operating the foot pedals and the other had his hands on the steering wheel. Ashok was horrified. We shrugged our shoulders, made the best of things and prayed that we would get to our destination in one piece! Godfrey was expecting to see Ashok, but he didn't know that I was coming as well. It was to be a welcome surprise for him.

Over the years of living and working in India, Calangute had been one of our favourite holiday places, where we could really relax and unwind. Goa is beautiful and Calangute, a little paradise beside the sea. The sunsets were spectacular, with the sky slowly going through all the colours of the rainbow which were reflected on the surface of the ocean. Most evenings would find us sitting on one of the beautiful, sandy beaches and watching a blood red sun gradually sinking down beyond the horizon. These moments were always a pleasure and filled my heart with great joy.

The Goans are mainly Catholic. Their little churches are very quaint and built in white-washed stone. Every day, the walls would turn to a most beautiful livid earthen colour in the heavenly sunsets. Many of the folk earned their living by fishing and they could be seen on the beaches with their little boats, pulling in and repairing their nets. The women, many of whom wear western style, brightly coloured, cotton dresses would also help the men mend the nets and haul in the fish whilst their little children ran around playing nearby.

Their music is lively and intoxicating with an exuberance that really lifts the spirits and was often being played loudly on the local buses as they passed by. The Goans always seemed to be happy. Finally, we dragged ourselves away from this paradise and travelled back up to Mussoorie, to pack our bags and leave for England.

readjustment

"...A song of the
Other world fills
My soul and
Fragments of melodies
Weave their subtle
Harmonies on
The mists of Time..."

(Poems from My Heart, 'Sunrise')

18 picking up the traces

ENGLAND WAS cold and grey. We missed the hot sunny days and clear blue skies to which we had grown accustomed in India. On arrival, we stayed with a great couple who ran a cosy little B&B and who treated us to outrageously delicious cream cakes on a fairly regular basis. They had a rotweiler dog called Cilla, who spent most of her time trying to sit on our laps and lick our faces. She was really sweet and shared our penchant for cream cakes!

We found a one-bedroom ground floor flat for sale in South Woodford and although it was very small, it was nicely decorated and cosy to live in. It was only a few hundred yards away from Epping Forest where I frequently walked amongst the trees, wondering where we would eventually end up. I started to paint again. The woodland inspired me. Epping Forest was a very healing place in which to be, yet I felt somewhat misplaced.

We found a comprehensive school for Charlie in Woodbridge and I joined a pottery class there. It was good to be doing something creative with hands on. Godfrey started his new teaching job and was offered a permanent post there, boosting his morale. However, we felt that we didn't want to live in such a built-up area. Properties were expensive and we needed more space. Nicolas also wanted to be back home with us. After living and working in Worcester, he had moved across and joined us for a while in this flat. He was not sure what he wanted to do. It was great that we were all back together again, but still minus the dog who was in quarantine. It was a bit of a tight squeeze in this flat but we were happy. I joined the local amateur orchestra and played the flute. I even managed to perform in a couple of concerts in the short time we were living there which cheered me up a little. As his temporary job was drawing to an end, Godfrey began to look around for a permanent post elsewhere and soon found one near Bath, where once my father had been at school. We all moved there in the summer of 1988. The school provided us with a house and a small garden which backed onto a car park at the rear of the school kitchens.

Kizzy joined us after her six months' quarantine, none the worse for her ordeal. When we went to collect her, all the staff came to wave goodbye to her! They had all loved her and had even put a photo of her up in their office.

Nicolas wanted a kitten and so we found one nearby from the Cat Protection League which had advertised in the local paper. She was a tiny, black and fluffy thing who was totally adorable and just about fitted on the palm of my hand. Nicolas was delighted. We called her Muffy. Slowly, she settled down to a new life with Kizzy who only just tolerated this new addition to the family. She was definitely the boss in our household. I had always felt that it was important for children to grow up with an animal around the place, so that they could learn about kindness and gentleness. I certainly had appreciated having animals around when I was growing up.

Nicolas eventually went off to college to study art and guess who ended up looking after the cat? One day, not very long after her arrival, she escaped out of the house and went missing for a good twenty-four hours. Eventually, she returned home badly beaten with both eyes very swollen and one completely closed. Later, we discovered that she had been attacked by the ginger tom who lived at the end of the car park as she was pregnant, eventually giving birth to three premature little kittens who died minutes after their birth.

That night, I went to bed wondering how I could help her heal her wounds while she slept in the kitchen along with Kizzy. As if in reply, I suddenly started to feel a tangible, hot energy building up in my solar plexus and so I started instinctively grabbing handfuls of this hot energy and, as I lay in bed, I visualised sending it down to her face. This heat seemed to radiate from the palm of my hand rather like a car headlight beam. No sooner had I taken one lot of energy from my solar plexus than it would start to build up again. It was amazing. This happened about half a dozen times. Afterwards, I felt exhausted and dropped off to sleep. An hour and a half later, I woke up to find the palms of my hands burning hot and prickly with sparks coming off them.

I jumped out of bed, went downstairs and put my hands on the cool earth outside in the garden. It was a clear night with a most beautiful full moon. The sparks and the heat disappeared instantly. Then I went back into the kitchen, putting the kettle on to make a cup of tea.

I looked down at Muffy, who was now busily rubbing her little body against my legs. She was purring and making a tremendous fuss. The swellings in her face had all gone, and her eyes seemed brighter than ever. She was completely healed. I was totally amazed. What was this energy that I had tapped into? This was the first intimation that I could give any healing.

Godfrey was happy with his new job and he became involved with the school boat club, training many of the boys to become successful oarsmen. The river was his sanctuary and coaching rowing helped him to settle back to life in the UK. We stayed in this beautiful area for nine years. The longest we had stayed anywhere.

Charlie started having drum lessons at his school in Oxfordshire. Ever since he had sat with the musicians at Kathak Kendra, he was interested in drumming. He enjoyed his classes and became a very good drummer. He eventually went to college, having successfully got onto a professional drumming course in London. Our two sons had left home. It was strange not having them around. Now, it was just the two of us. Charlie inspired me so much with his drumming that I also started having drum lessons and I bought a seven-piece kit, then joined a jazz workshop that met regularly in Bath.

I discovered that I had a reasonable sense of rhythm and also joined a Samba band. The Bath group got together with the Bristol Samba band and twenty seven of us went to play at Glastonbury Festival, the annual three-day international music festival. During the three days, we didn't get much chance of sleep. The fact that we all survived at all was probably due to the tequila slammers we were given at fairly regular intervals!

15 a glimpse of truth

WE ENJOYED the social activities of the school and made some good friends in the area. But I had not found that ultimate peace. I felt a constant underlying restlessness and confusion. I had seen many great yogis, buddhist monks, holy men and all kinds of people in my life, doing all kinds of rituals and austerities . . . searching for that missing ingredient. Had they not found it? I remember some hadn't looked particularly happy. In fact, many of them had looked decidedly grim! What was it all about anyway? I knew that there was something else . . .

I thought about the Dzogchen teachings again. It would be interesting to meet the Dzogchen master, Namkhai Norbu, who had written the book I had been given by Shalini in Delhi. Then another memory slipped in . . . It was my old friend. He had sat down beside me, on our favourite log in a little bit of the woodland in the garden, where everything was quiet except for the usual rustling of leaves and the smell of the wood that were so familiar.

'My darling child,' he said, 'Truth is—where there is Silence. Silence of speech, silence of sight, silence of sound and especially, silence of mind.'

I was entranced . . .

He continued. 'We can always stop talking, go quiet, speechless and be peaceful. If we choose, we need not look here and there, restless, searching everywhere out there in the world. It's easy to be silent right here, now, wherever we are. We can keep our mouths shut. We do not need to look, as we can close our eyes. We also need not listen. We can block our ears. But if we think of stillness of the mind . . . . .'

'But,' I interrupted, 'how can we still the mind? It is constantly chattering away. I am always thinking. It isn't possible to shut off the thoughts!'

He smiled, 'Now there's a thought. It is true that we have so many thoughts coming and going. But our mind is actually made up of thoughts. Did you know that it is **just** a bundle of thoughts? You are right, it is totally impossible to silence our mind, but we can choose to take no notice of the thoughts and not be attached to them.'

I remembered asking my dear old friend to tell me about these thoughts.

'Thoughts . . . .' he had said, and he had laughed so much! He had gone silent for quite a long time before becoming very serious . . . . Then he spoke.

'My dear, just for a moment, imagine a very calm lake with not a ripple or a bubble to be seen. You are sitting on the bank. The sky is blue. There are little white clouds slowly floating by. You see the clouds reflected on the calm surface of the lake.

'These clouds are a bit like our thoughts, in that they are always coming and going. This is the nature of our thoughts. To come and go.

'The surface of the lake is completely unaffected whatever happens on it.

'We cannot put our hand into the lake and remove the clouds any more than we can erase our thoughts. All we'll succeed in doing is agitating the water and in turn, we agitate the reflected clouds, just as we are constantly agitating our minds with our thoughts. Nevertheless, we can see that these clouds are there reflected perfectly on the still water, but the surface of the water is not touched in any way. It can never be tainted by any of these reflections. This untainted, unruffled condition is our pure, natural state. In the same way, our thoughts cannot touch our natural state. But can we say that they do not exist? We cannot remove them, but we **can** choose not to identify with them.'

'I think I am almost getting it. Okay, so I have understood that we cannot silence our mind because its nature is to "think" all the time. But what we can do is to let the thoughts just be and not get involved with them. Take absolutely no notice of them, then they will just come and go, rather like the clouds reflected on the smooth surface of the lake, and not disturb us. Have I understood you correctly?'

'Yes, dearest, that is right. You have understood well. Then, and only then will we have peace.' And then he laughed.

'But is it possible ever really to be silent or to have peace . . . . .?' I asked.

'Yes', he said, 'when we discover non-attachment.'

'What *is* non-attachment?' I asked.

He said, 'Non-attachment is not being attached or "clinging" to anything at all!'

'Anything at all?' I asked, surprised.

Then he leaned over and whispered in a very quiet way. 'When consciousness looks at itself, it does not become attached to itself because it just is!'

'What do you mean?' I asked.

He replied quietly, 'If you can become an observer, a witness, who doesn't judge anything at all, you can just experience everything without interfering or getting involved. An impartial observer is someone who does not . . . speak with judgment, look with judgment, listen with judgment or think judging thoughts.'

I said, 'Judgment, what is that?'

'Just our opinion, which is usually based on past events or future hopes,' he said.

'Whose opinion?' I asked.

'Exactly!' he laughed.

'Ummmm...,' I thought to myself.

Then he told me a little story . . .

'There is an old Hindu legend which tells how at the beginning of time, this world was created by Brahma, the God of Creation, from the Source of pure cosmic energy. Everything was beautiful and pure. It was supremely light, full of love and unconditionality.'

'What do you mean by unconditionality?' I interrupted.

'Well, everything to do with this world, just was.'

'What do you mean—just *was*?'

'Well, there was no up nor down, neither good nor bad, no he or she . . .'

'But that is how we define the world as we know it. We can only know it by its opposites!' I said.

'You are right,' he replied, 'and in order for the world to be defined in this way, it had to come from somewhere else—or so you think! I will explain.

'In those days the oceans were full of beautiful water beings and the skies were full of beautiful bird beings and celestials (angels), who sang all the time. On the surface of the earth lived many kinds of creatures who lived happily and contentedly together.

'At this time, all human beings were gods, but, sadly, they began to abuse their divinity to such an extent that Brahma had to step in and do something about it.

'He decided to take their divine power away from them. The problem was, where to hide it. So he summoned the lesser gods from all the universes to come together for a meeting, as He had to discuss and resolve this very serious problem with them.

'The big day arrived and all the gods of all the realms and universes came and met with the Lord of Creation. Lord Brahma's voice boomed out and around the great hall. Everyone was alert, expectant and very silent.

'Out of our great wisdom and compassion,' He said, "I have called you all to help Me resolve an extremely serious problem that has come to My attention.'

'Whatever can that be?' somebody asked.

'The divine human race has seriously misused its divinity and I have had to take it away from them and now I need to find a good hiding place for it so that only those who are serious and have the right motivation can rediscover their true identity.

'Now, what we have got to do is to decide amongst ourselves how and where we should hide this spark of divinity, this little drop from the source of bliss and cosmic energy.'

There followed much intense discussion and heated excitement about where this spark of divinity should be placed, so that the human beings who were really serious about discovering peace for themselves could actually find it. For several weeks this debating continued.

One suggested that the spark of divinity be hidden in the deepest forest.

Someone else said, 'No, no! - The humans might exploit the forests, and sell the wood for profit. They would surely do the same with this treasure.'

Then somebody else suggested, 'How about in the deepest ocean?'

'Oh no! They would go fishing and diving, plunging the depths deeper and deeper for more and more profit and discover the spark of divinity and auction it for self gain.'

Someone else had a bright idea and suggested 'the highest mountain,' and again the response was 'No, no, no! It would be too easy, for the humans would climb the highest heights to search for this spark of divinity so that they could win fame and fortune!'

And so it went on and on.

Now amongst this gathering of gods and great beings, there were some who really stood head and shoulders above the rest in their infinite wisdom and compassion.

Lord Shiva was there for a start and during all this time, he had remained silent. He stood up, and surveyed the mighty crowd. Everyone was hushed. Not a sound could be heard when He spoke.

'O great assembly! I have listened to all of your discussions.

'I have listened to all your debating and deliberations.

'I have only this one thing to say.

'Place this spark of divinity in the sacred heart-space of each and every human being. They will never think of looking there.'

Sheer genius. What a wonderful idea! Everyone agreed and cheered and cheered. Yes indeed. This was by far the very best place possible. A sigh of great relief went through the crowd.

And so it was done.

Thus it was brought about that from that moment in the dim distant past to this very day, human beings, who were originally gods, now have the opportunity to re-discover for themselves, if they really are serious enough, that they are pure consciousness itself, which is—who they truly are. That they are truly divine!

There was a long silence before either of us had spoken. I had loved that story. His words were still wandering around in my head...

'Well, let's go back to where we started from, and explore that word—silence . . .

'Silence is our teacher. Silence leads us to compassion and wisdom, and our words will slowly become more loving and meaningful. They will be full of clarity because they will be coming from the Source, that very ocean of bliss and cosmic energy—which is consciousness, as you know.'

'So, what you are saying is that if I spoke less and became more silent, I would find out who I am?'

'Indeed!'

'Okay. I shall try to be very quiet.'

'But, you know, this is not enough,' he continued. 'When we turn inwards, we start to see with "inner" eyes and hear with "inner" ears. The mind turned inwards, eventually goes very, very quiet. That's when it all becomes rather interesting. As soon as we are quiet, we may begin to notice that we have no thoughts in particular. Then, if we show absolutely no interest in them, we will not be brought into any kind of conflict or discussion with them. Now, the trick is to try and stay in this place of quietness. But the moment we start paying attention to our thoughts and begin dialoguing with them, that is the beginning of all our troubles.

'All thoughts arise from our own personal "I" thought, I am this, I have that etc, etc. In fact, that is the very root of all thoughts; This "I" thought. Think about it. You are so close to understanding this, my dearest.'

I remembered being in a total spin about all that he had told me. My old companion from my childhood days had been so wise. When I think about all the things he had shared with me all those years ago, I wondered if he was even real! I had never met anyone else who had such clear knowledge of all spiritual matters. He had spoken of the one-ness of everything, but somehow, I was still wasting my time searching around trying to find it.

Had I learned nothing over the years?

'Clear your mind of attachment to all your thoughts. Recognise that you are the Truth.

Readjustment

'You are all that is. And everything is just as it should be, good and bad . . . . .' His words continued to weave their magic in the back of my mind somewhere . . . . .

Over the years, I had kept notebooks of poems and inspirational insights as they came to me and I had also kept a dream journal. These were all accounts of how I felt and what I perceived was happening to me in those special moments. As I looked back on them, there was a thread of continual 'longing'. Longing for that ultimate embrace, that ultimate taste . . . when I would actually 'recognise' and really *know* and experience Truth. I was willing to explore any avenue that would lead me to *that* for which I was yearning.

20 mandalas

"...The centre that I cannot find,

Is known to my Unconscious mind;

I have no reason to despair

Because I am already there."

(Auden, 'The Labyrinth')

I WAS introduced to Mandalas and the art of Mandala painting through a friend of a friend who painted them for her own discovery, self knowledge and therapy. I was fascinated. Mandalas are beautiful designs, done in a circle or spiral. This is because the whole of life is like one big circle or cycle. Their origins are to be found way back in the ancient mists of time and in most spiritual traditions around the world. In each spiritual system they are recreated through meditation and ritual through the use of symbols which represent our life in so many meaningful ways.

Through the Mandala, I began a journey into an inner world towards my own spiritual centre like an inward throw of a small pebble into the pool of one's own brilliant consciousness. It was absorbing and fascinating.

I discovered that Mandalas were a powerful focus for developing concentration and how great they were at helping me to re-discover my own sense of self worth, when I approached them in the right way. They taught me a lot about Truth as I began to tune into their divine nature and how they re-established me in the centre of my being.

I discovered that Mandalas were complete in themselves. That they seemed to 'embody' the whole of life. That is, they were complete *only* if they met certain criteria. The first, being a 'centre' (which is unmanifested potential), the second, 'manifestation' (potential being manifested), then the 'individual' (the experiencer), the third, space (the 'ground' on which the manifestation moves outwards), and finally, time (continuity).

I experimented and worked with Mandalas on my own at home over a period of four years and many of my problems and doubts were overcome in this way.

I had a lot of insights and fun, re-discovering and re-defining myself. Slowly, a surreptitious light began to enter my heart. It was all very quiet and subtle. Some major shifts happened within me, and I really felt that I could trust the process . . .

Then a flashback intruded into my consciousness, to a conversation that I had had with my old friend . . . He turned up at our home once, in a horse-drawn cart. It was Easter and he had brought us some chocolate eggs. He was always doing kind things and telling me funny stories. He lifted me up onto the cart and off we trotted down the little lanes that ran around our village. He was talking about circles and space . . .

'Life is like a circle. It goes around and comes around.'

'What do you mean?' I said.

He replied, 'Day and night. They come and go regularly. I come and visit you, then I go away again. The sea ebbs and flows, doesn't it? We are born and eventually we will die. Just now, we left your house and we are going around and around the lanes and finally we will return to the house.' Then he started to speak in a very serious voice. I was totally absorbed by what he said.

'In the very centre of our being, is a tiny "space." (It is not really a proper "space" at all, because it really cannot be put into words properly or be seen clearly by the naked eye.) It is a space with no dimensions or definitions. It is not a space in the real sense of the word. It is more . . . a state of . . . stillness. In this place of space is the very fabric of who we are and what we are made of. This is what I call pure consciousness, or pure awareness. Our "definition" or personality is born out of this space. This space always is and always has been and will always be. It is really indefineable.

'Now, I know how much you love to dance, so I will use the example that we are all like dancers, who spin and spiral out from our centre, creating and re-creating our form.

'From this centre we manifest myriad things. Just as the spider sits and weaves her world around her, in the same way we weave our world and wrap ourselves in this creation. Then we sit in the centre of this, our created world and get thoroughly caught up in all those things we have created, dreaming and believing that this is it, that this is our true life, never for a moment thinking that this could possibly be just a mere reflection . . . of the actual truth.

'This centre is the empty space from which all is born (becomes visible) and from which all will die (become invisible). But the actual space itself is pure consciousness, which is not visible or invisible.

'Where is that empty space when all we do is fill it up with our own junk? How can we say, "It is not there?" and tell me, who is it that says that, anyway?'

Umm. What a fantastic thought. And if it were true? He often used to say 'and **who is it** that is doing or saying something?' What did he mean, I wondered to myself?

He continued, 'Interestingly, this space is to be found in the centre of all wheels. Let's go and have a little look.' He stopped speaking for a moment, halted the pony, arranged the reins and then we climbed down from the cart and looked at the wheels. They were funny old wheels with rusty spokes in them, but, yes, there was a fixed point right in the middle of each of the wheels. This is how they were designed. I hadn't ever taken much notice of how wheels were made. 'It is this very little space that allows the wheels to turn. Even if we could not see this actual space, there would still be a point of no movement from which the wheel would turn, otherwise it would not be able to turn at all.

'When we start looking inwards, to inside ourselves, we will re-discover that space. This empty space is our proper centre. From this is made manifest all that there is to be known. We can manifest it or withdraw it at will. Doesn't the spider withdraw her weavings back within herself if she so wishes? From this empty space, we create all that there is in our lives. From this empty space, we create and choose all that happens to us. From the very fabric of **that which is**, we are formed, could we but understand it. Hidden within this empty space is all our potential. How could we wish to be "this" or to do "that" when we already **are** it? That is, pure consciousness.'

I thought long and hard about this. I hadn't understood much of what he was talking about at the time and I was forever asking him questions.

'So, what you are saying is that we are pure consciousness, but I don't really understand what "pure consciousness" is?'

With that familiar twinkle in his eyes, he replied, 'Pure consciousness is energy, pure energy which is manifested as different vibrations. If we had some special scientific equipment so that we could see it all, we would soon discover that we were made up of billions of tiny atoms and so forth. We are actually not solid at all—just vibrations moving at different speeds. If we were to use the same equipment, we would also see that everything else around us was also made up of atoms and such like. Things only look solid because our normal vision limits us.'

What an amazing thought, I pondered. Here we are, having been born from this space which is already within us, then gradually we find ourselves living this 'life' that we have created all by ourselves, believing that this is all there is, because we have somehow lost our connection with that space which is within us.

I asked him, 'Then this space that we are talking about is also pure consciousness and we are just a small part of the greatest secret you once told me about. This so called great secret is no secret at all really then, is it?'

'No,' he said. 'that is exactly right.'

We create and choose everything in our lives that happens to us, both good and bad from that small centre within ourselves. Yes, I thought, this is that 'spark of divinity' in the story he once told me. It is the same. We forget the centre (inside ourselves) and only see the outer bit, thinking that this is all there is. So, I continued to play and experiment with the Mandalas. The journey started with a white sheet of paper. There it was: a blank space, just an empty space . . . This *empty space* represented Source or Truth for me. That blissful ocean of nectar that I had occasionally sensed .

I sat still, very quiet. Full of potential . . . without any limitations...

Here, I discovered, there were infinite possibilities . . . In this place of emptiness, of infinite potential, *Truth* could really speak to me. Here, no questions could arise as already I was *'That'* . . . if only I could experience it. I discovered that if, from this place of no-thing, no-time, no-space . . . I was to put my paint-brush onto this blank sheet, loaded with any beautiful colour . . . of *my* choice, then started to paint . . . something very interesting and magical began to happen.

I discovered that whatever I *chose*, this was the way I defined myself . . . All this came from my still-point centre. Then I moved outwards into *being*—that is into the world of manifestation. I started to define myself by the *'colours'* (influences) of my environment, my associations, my family, my friends. I had the choice to paint and design whatever and however I wished. This was really exciting.

So now, having moved away with my paint brush from my still-point centre, I asked myself, *'Who is This who is painting . . .?'* the answer was 'It is me.' I had now successfully become a . . . somebody . . . This was like a bomb-shell! I could see now through the painting of the Mandala, that I had very clearly labelled myself as to what and who I thought I was. I discovered that I had totally limited myself. I was well and truly defined and curtailed. I now understood that I lived in a world of names and forms . . . In short, duality. I found out that I could make a most beautiful design or a not-so-beautiful one, depending on my personal choice of colours, etc. This could be likened to my outer world of choices.

Yes, I certainly had choices. I could *choose* to do or to be whoever I liked. I could choose to get myself into trouble or not. In short, I could choose any situation I wished, whenever and however, I liked. Wow, this was an extraordinary discovery. From this, I knew that I could also choose . . . . Freedom! I discovered, that I created my own reality just like creating my own design in a Mandala. It all came out from that still-point centre inside me as and when I chose. I discovered too, that if I reversed this whole process and went *back* to that still-point centre, that place of full potential, (the empty space), I could definitely return to the state of non-being, to that state of non-duality where no-thing is defined . . . . . Just as the spider weaves and spins its own cobweb then lives in it, by the same token it could also ingest its web back to within itself . . .

I had inadvertently stumbled across the knowledge that there was no *becoming* to become. I did not have to go and search 'out there', or anywhere 'else' to find the truth. All the time it is right here, right now, *wherever* I am. I am, in fact, *that* which is doing the looking. I had to *Be* the experience . . . I now understood that the present moment of *Now* is the eternal experience that all the sages and saints had so frequently spoken about.

Mandalas were a visual aid for me to understand *that* which was impossible to comprehend with any 'normal' rational, thinking, mind process.

ONE DAY, I met a remarkable woman called Nancy who had been a Bahá'í for a long time. She was spiritually mature and we became good friends. I adored her. We often met in the centre of Bath and over numerous cups of coffee we had long conversations about Truth. I just loved our talks on spiritual things and these meetings nourished my soul.

Originally, Nancy had trained and worked as a university counsellor. She now worked with a few organisations in the area, helping many different people with all kinds of problems. This friend was incredibly authentic and wise. I trusted her implicitly and she had a wonderfully loving way with her choice of words whenever she was talking to me.

During my life, I felt that I could never properly express what my heart was really wanting to say. As children, we had not been allowed a voice. We were not allowed to express our feelings and thoughts and we were never encouraged to have discussions about anything, so I guess that my inability to say what I really wanted to say was possibly due to this. If I was wanting to be sympathetic to someone, it always felt as if the words came out in a clumsy way. I was impressed by how she communicated with everyone. She was very skilled with all those she met and I tried hard to emulate her way of being.

To me, she represented the universal, wise and loving Mother. Many other people around loved her too. She seemed to embody a compassion for others that came from a totally unconditional place. She was an illumined soul who loved all human beings completely. I must admit that over the years, I had often preferred animals to humans. I knew that I would always love animals; that there is a place for them too in the great scheme of things, but to love them *more* than other humans . . . I wondered why? Was it because they didn't answer back? I don't know. Eventually, I soon began to think that maybe it was my way of not facing up to myself. It was true that I did not trust myself at all, so how could I trust others? This, I discovered, was the 'home grown' projection of my own fears. I needed to be more in touch with the real 'me'. Then maybe I could also begin to love humanity better. Maybe, the words I spoke would also come out in a more meaningful way.

This friend was a breath of fresh air for me in all those days of questioning. She so completely inspired me, that I would often think of her whenever I was talking to somebody in need, inwardly asking her for inspiration to say the most beneficial and appropriate thing needed at that moment.

She had a personal vision of a much greater reality than that given to us by any organised religion. It was this quality that had first attracted me to her. I knew from my own spiritual enquiry and journey that we all needed to have these qualities that she possessed in order to reach the source of our desires.

Through Nancy, I met quite a few interesting people and once, she had a young American woman staying in her home. This lady was into planetary healing amongst other things. She organized a group meditation for healing the planet, to be held in Nancy's home and to which I was invited. This was held on the occasion of the '11.11', which was a time of opening the 'portals' to the outer universe. This was a very auspicious time for bringing positive energies into the planet that would help to heal it. About a dozen people were there, and it was during this meditation that I was to have my first direct experience of *non-duality*, although at the time I didn't fully appreciate or understand it.

As she led us all through a beautiful creative visualisation meditation, I listened quietly . . . Her American accent was slow and gentle. I followed in great detail exactly everything she was saying in the meditation . . . . The next thing I knew was that I was flying over all the continents of the world, one by one, crossing each of the great oceans and pouring a red-coloured dust out of my hands over all the areas of the earth and seas. I was somehow not 'me' any more. I had the feeling of all-embracing power and my ego personality had dissolved. It felt like 'I' was just an energy of some sort. 'I' saw the mountains and the rivers. This 'I' somehow seemed to 'know' about all the happinesses and the sadnesses of human beings and the suffering of all living creatures. 'I' saw forest fires, murders, terrible cruelties and the ugliness of wars. At the same time, this 'I' saw the love in a mother's gentle caress for her child; a child hugging a dog; the beauty of the forests and all of nature in her majestic splendour; the loving caresses of man for woman; the kindnesses done just for the sheer pleasure of being kind . . . 'I' saw the totality of all existence here, everywhere on this truly amazing and beautiful planet. The astonishing thing was that 'I' felt an all-encompassing, total compassion and an extraordinary, impersonal love for every single living thing that was witnessed. There was no sense of judgment. It all just was as it was and the feeling was peaceful and expansive. There was no sense of a doer doing anything at all. It was as if my 'I'-ness was an intricate part of the whole of the universe.

Afterwards, I wanted to know what it all meant . . . but no-one there seemed to be able to answer my questions. Nobody had understood what had happened to me . . .

22 empowerment

THROUGH MY contact with various people in and around Bath, I was invited to join a group of women who meditated regularly in the Sulis hot baths and springs in the centre of the town. I was considered a resident of Bath although we lived just outside and I was allowed to use the facilities freely.

One day, I had gone down to the meditation gathering as usual, but this time the authorities wouldn't let me in, saying that I was no longer considered a resident, as the boundary line had been moved to include just the city of Bath itself, therefore I would have to pay. I had come without my purse, so I sat on a bench outside feeling somewhat dejected. A little while later, one of the group members came along and suggested that I make myself invisible, then I could just walk in and join the rest of them.

Invisible? What an amazing thought. How could I do that? I was fascinated by the idea of becoming invisible! So she described to me how to do it. First of all, I had to go very, very quiet and disconnect myself from my ego-self. I had to imagine that all my thoughts and my 'being-me-ness'—that is, my personality—were being withdrawn from the outer world to within my own being. A bit like a spider ingesting her web back into herself. Then I would not be seen, simply because my aura or my energy field had also been withdrawn.

My 'I-ness' would have been removed. The man on the door would not be able to 'sense' or to be aware of my energy field passing by. Here, I was being asked to actually put the theory of the Mandala into practice. Could I do it? Could I recreate my reality?

I sat for a few moments and focused as I withdrew my ego personality, my 'I-ness'. Then I got up and proceeded to walk . . . right past the guard with this friend. We were not seen. I had done it. What an extraordinary thing. It really worked. I was amazed. The power of our mind is so incredible. All I had to do was to trust that I could do it. I really had to believe in myself. If I trusted in that underlying eternal consciousness, or God, or whatever I wanted to call it, I could do anything I wished to do.

Later, I wondered if I had done the right thing by getting in for free when I should have paid. But then, I thought to myself, they were the ones who had changed the rules . . . but was it still right for me to do it? I wondered about this for quite some time afterwards.

As we had been given a house with Godfrey's job we were now in a position to buy a place of our own somewhere else. We thought it would be good to keep a little place, even if it was just as a holiday home. So when we sold our flat in South Woodford, we went house hunting. We were introduced to an interesting Bahá'í couple who lived in Mid Wales, called Meg and Greg. They had three children, and sometimes offered Bed and Breakfast, so we booked in with them for a few days whilst we looked around the area. They lived in Cymystwyth, which was the first village one came across, having traversed the very beautiful Rhyader mountain road. We found a great little place in the village of Pontrhydygroes with fantastic views over the Ystwyth valley. This village had one small shop with a few houses scattered around. It was a good place to go, and we often saw beautiful red kites flying high in the sky.

We escaped to this paradise whenever Godfrey managed to take the time out from his hectic work routine.We found we had a lot in common with Meg and Greg and we became good friends. Once we had moved in, we frequently met up and went for long walks altogether. The extensive Hafod Estate was not very far away and offered some fifty miles of excellent rambles and views. It was a beautiful spot and full of bird song. In the grounds, there had been a very large mansion which had been burned down a long time ago and never re-built, which seemed a pity. Eventually, even the ruins had been pulled down.

On the estate, there was a cave known as Robbers' Cave, which we liked to visit as it always provided a good walk. It could only be reached by going through the forest and along a high, steep ridge. The cave itself had actually been created by blasting into the rock face so that one could enter right into it and come face to face with a high waterfall which flowed constantly down the rock face opposite. It was a most beautiful and peaceful spot and there was an interesting energy there.

Once, while I was standing quietly in the cave watching the waterfall, I became aware of a presence near me. I looked across to my right and saw to my surprise, an extremely thin, old woman dressed in a long, black dress, with bare white arms and feet. What was really noticeable was the fact that her face was about half the usual width of any normal human being. She looked stern but immediately she smiled at me and seemed pleased that I was giving this place respect. I did not move and we communicated with smiles in utter silence until eventually she disappeared as quickly and as quietly as she had appeared. I assumed that she was the guardian of the cave.

Another time, we had walked across some woodlands in the Hafod Estate with our friends when we approached a smaller waterfall flowing into a stream. We decided to take a short rest and we all sat around, each in our own space, not talking but just enjoying each other's company and the glorious sunny day. The birds were singing and the sound of the water created a tranquil atmosphere all around me . . . I sat still.

Suddenly it all began with a little feeling of expansion. My awareness started reaching out in all directions. My ego personality seemed to expand too, to such a point that it disappeared. This expansive awareness continued to extend, taking in all the sounds, smells and views of the waterfall, stream, hills, woodlands, the sky and everything else that surrounded me. It was as if I had become one with everything, as if my I-ness had merged with them all; that my 'consciousness' had become the consciousness of everything else around me. The feeling was of inconceivable vastness . . . as if my consciousness was alive with all the consciousnesses of everything else around . . . as if I was the very life of the grasses, of the stones, of all things. I had 'become' the stream, 'become' the waterfall. I was actually the sound of the wind in the trees. I had become as unmoving as the hills and was as empty as the vast skies. In fact, it was as if I was 'being' in the 'becoming' of all things. It was a feeling that I *'was'* everything . . . There was only what I could describe, as an *'eternity'* of everything. A sort of seamless state with no beginning and no end. An eternal moment! Who knows how long it lasted? Something inside me felt that this might be an experience of the 'natural' state. Was this the truth? I gently felt the presence of my old childhood friend beside me, and knew that he had understood what had happened to me just then . . .

Meg had become interested in the spiritual teachings of the Medicine Wheel, which is the sacred path of the Native Americans. She talked to me about a teacher who occasionally came over from the United States to give shamanic teachings from this ancient sacred path. She was soon going to be coming to the area, to give some workshops called 'The Children's Fire.' Would I like to go? We could go together.

These teachings were about connecting with the Great Spirit (the Divine) and healing the child within, through working with the various aspects of Mother Nature. Everything in nature is necessarily a teacher and healer. Understanding this could be helpful in showing us how to live more fully in our personal daily life. The rocks could teach us. Even the flowers, the trees, the birds and all the creatures were teachers. The elements were also messengers for us to come to know and understand Great Spirit.

These teachings included discovering who our own personal totem animal or bird was. This animal or bird could appear to us in the 'dreamtime' or through our personal meditations. They had qualities that could teach us how to live in a more complete and harmonious way with everybody and everything around us. These animals or birds could also protect us in times of danger.

This sounded very interesting, so I decided to go.

When the time came, I prepared myself for a short camping weekend and off we both went to this Medicine Wheel gathering, which was being held in some fields on a large farm not so far away from our little Welsh home. I had no idea what to expect and I went with a fairly open mind. On our arrival, there was quite a big crowd of people who were already establishing themselves in their various tents and camper vans around the site. And so we also prepared ourselves for the forthcoming event.

In the middle of the field was a large, painted hogan (tent), which had been erected for the occasion, large enough to hold everybody comfortably sitting in a circle. In the centre was a big fire and through the top of the tent was a hole with a flap where the smoke could go out.

I was a little apprehensive and had no idea what to expect. For some reason, the teacher was very harsh towards me. I couldn't do anything right or so it seemed at the time. I found this hard to cope with and became very upset. Some kind person consoled me somewhat by saying that this was how she taught some people. Especially if they suffered from the 'poor me' syndrome. I must say, that at this point, I was definitely feeling sorry for myself!

However, I have always considered myself a survivor and I used the time constructively, by really taking the opportunity to look at my past. There were others around me who were also having a difficult time and I felt sorry for them too. As a child, I had been raised with a lot of harshness and I needed to really look at this issue as I saw it and then deal with it. I needed to forgive, which also included forgiving myself. I needed to sever the negative aspects and move on. I did not want to spend the rest of my life feeling sorry for myself. I also had a thought that I did not want to die still feeling antagonistic and resentful towards my parents. In short, I wanted and needed healing. It was truly 'The Children's Fire'.

The intensity of the weekend was exactly what I needed and towards the end, the teacher took the time to speak to me. My negative feelings and anger just seemed to 'dissolve' and she filled this 'void' with a lot of energy. I felt re-empowered and ready to start the rest of my life without regrets.

But there was to be one more event that I would take part in before I left . . .

I was already feeling better about myself. My attitude towards my parents was definitely inproving. I no longer cried when I thought or spoke about them as I had always done up to this point because they had affected me so much. I had released the bad memories of the past and I began to look at my parents with the eye of detachment. My emotional body felt less damaged. More and more, I realised that my parents would never change. It was me who had to change! I just did not need to respond in the way I always had done before. I was learning the technique of releasing the anger and pain that so persistently attached itself to me. The secret seemed to be in not 're-acting' to their controlling strategies. I was not going to resort to the usual responses provoked by the past conditioning of my mind. I had discovered something very important. My mind was the creator of all my troubles! But my mind could also be the healer of all these troubles too.

At the end of the weekend gathering, we were all invited to stay on if we wished, to take part in a 'vision quest'. This was to be the extra event.

This particular vision quest entailed us being alone somewhere on the land over a twenty-four hour period in the place of our choosing. We would be connecting with nature, Spirit, and our inner selves. Out of the large group, only six of us decided to stay on. It was not an easy decision for me to make, given the way things had been during the weekend, but I was keen for change and had felt so 'stuck' in many aspects of my life. Now I was beginning to feel that things could move on and this is what I really wanted. This was another opportunity . . . Besides, I was always up for an adventure!

After the others had gone, the six of us who remained met with the teacher in the Hogan. We were then told what we would need to do. We all went out to find our personal quiet 'place'. Having located my spot in the middle of a very large, hilly field, I started to build my medicine circle with smallish stones that I had collected earlier. This took a long time, as each stone had to be 'asked' for permission first, before taking it. This act taught us that everything around us is sacred and we should not abuse our natural habitat. In the same way, each stone was lovingly and thoughtfully laid down in its correct place and represented the various different aspects of my nature. Every stone was connected to the four elements and to the various guardians of the four directions. Each direction of the medicine wheel represented life-changing opportunities for me and I really hoped for some great changes for the better in my life after this. We had also been told to bring along some tobacco which we sprinkled around the outer periphery of the circle and to use some as an offering to the Great Spirit.

Once it was built, I sat down in the centre, well wrapped up in warm clothing, wearing a woolly hat and waterproof boots. I had a few extra belongings which included a torch, an old sleeping bag and a large black dustbin bag to sit in, in case it rained. I also had a banana, some dry biscuits and water to drink to keep me going.

For the first couple of hours, I cried and cried my heart out. I wondered what on earth I was doing there sitting in the middle of a field all on my own. So many thoughts were bombarding me and I felt very afraid. I chose this site as I thought that I would be able to see everything around me. The fact was that I could. Unfortunately, the down-side was that I was also as conspicuous as an elephant sitting on a park bench. Finally, I was enclosed in my not very large, stone circle which had taken hours to build and there was no way out. We had all been told earlier that we should not leave our circles until the very end of the twenty four hours if possible. I was determined to see it through to the end.

Sitting there, I was totally exposed to all the elements that the skies could chuck at me. Was I mad? In this circle, I faced all my demons. I called all my medicine animals to be with me and I sang a lot. I chanted all kinds of prayers. One of them was a Bahá'í prayer I knew, which I found was very powerful and I repeated it over and over like a mantra for my protection. It worked. Slowly, I began to embrace all those fears that were haunting and taunting me throughout the darkness of the night. The strange thing was I discovered that as soon as I really faced them, they disappeared right before my very eyes! One minute they were seemingly very real and threatening and the next, they had totally gone and all the negative feelings had gone with them. It was a most extraordinary thing. The message was clear: Face them then embrace them . . . then they would be no more. Gone. I became quite fearless and this was very empowering.

At some point during the night it rained very hard and the air became quite cold. I snuggled deeply into my sleeping bag within the large black plastic bag and tried to keep as dry as I could and wondered how the others were faring.

Many strange things happened during the night and I was to witness a unusual event. I was looking up into the clear night sky and could just make out the dark outlines of some tall trees nearby. Then I saw what looked like a huge spaceship. It was partially hidden behind the trees. I could see lights flashing horizontally around a dark spherical shape which extended way beyond the trees and I seriously did not want to be beamed up! I had read so much in the past about abductions and all kinds of weird things around sightings of UFO's that my imagination started to get the better of me. I sat and stared at it and surrounded myself in light, hoping that it would help. Eventually, it disappeared as suddenly as it had appeared. Did it really exist or was it just a figment of my imagination?

The moment the sun began to rise, my heart sang for joy. It was such a beautiful sight to behold. Now, we would be able to leave our circles, dismantling them in a sacred way and returning the stones back to their natural habitat.

The six of us gathered back in the Hogan to meet the teacher. She was pleased that no-one had left their circles. We shared some of the experiences that we had encountered. I discovered that someone else had seen that spacecraft too. I had achieved what I had set out to do. I was very pleased with myself for having stuck it out. This weekend was a real turning point for me. I was changing. I could see a brighter future.

Afterwards, I drove back to our little cottage in Pontrhydygroes, had a hot bath and felt a whole heap better and clean once again. I decided to drive straight back to Bath. The drive home was to be one of the most difficult drives of my life. One that I wouldn't want to repeat in a hurry. I was almost half-way home and not feeling too bad or so I thought. But after a few miles, I felt a real deep-seated tiredness beginning to overtake me which was not surprising as I hadn't slept for twenty-four hours. I veered onto the wrong side of the road several times, having dozed off, and that was really scary. Luckily for me, the roads were pretty empty and I reached home in one piece, totally exhausted but safe and sound, just as Godfrey was getting up to go to work. He was very surprised to see me back so soon. He made me a cup of tea, then I went to bed and slept for the rest of the day.

I continued working with this teacher for a while and did a sweat lodge with her. This was my first experience of a sweat lodge. It was rather like sitting in a sauna but much hotter. During the session, my vision turned completely upside down and I had to leave the tent. I lay down for a while and felt as if I was dying, as the heat of my body and the cool of the outside air met, but it was a pleasant feeling, and I was looked after by a very caring person as I recovered.

I began filling my life with positive affirmations and to help me with this, I had several animal 'totem' friends who helped me from the dimension of Spirit. One was a very beautiful brown bear. This bear taught me about looking within. 'Bear' medicine taught me about the 'sweetness' of Truth and of silence in retreat. At different times, the totem animals would change. I had a swan who stayed with me for some time. Swan was about transforming my negative thought patterns into constructive opportunities and she taught me that change was always possible. I also had an eagle for a while. He taught me about freedom and openness and learning how to see the greater picture; to 'rise above' the difficulties. He taught me about choices I could make because, from this perspective, I could see more clearly. A wolf stayed a while too. Wolves are great teachers to their young and wolf medicine taught me about the teacher inside myself. I knew that I always loved to share information with others.

Another time, I had a very large, beautiful seagull dream along with me! He taught me to be bold so that I could feel more confident in my choices in life. I had a few others too at different times and each creature that visited me stood for a particular quality and aspect that I needed to work with at the time. In fact, at any time I found that I could call upon any of these beautiful creatures and they would instantly be there ready and willing to help me. I was so grateful for their support.

Over the next few months, I participated in other sweat lodges and Medicine Wheel workshops with different teachers. One was held in Gloucestershire, in the company of the late Sun Bear, who was a famous Native American teacher and healer. He was the head of the Bear Tribe and he often came to the UK to share the sacred teachings.

I acquired one of Sun Bear's medicine pipes in a most magical way. It was a gift, as these things always are. I had become a pipe carrier, and this was considered a very special honour and I took it very seriously. I made a special bag for it. Later, I was to smoke this peace pipe in ceremony with two other beautiful women whom I had had the privilege to meet at these gatherings. One of them had been responsible for my acquisition of the peace pipe, along with a rainbow-coloured sweater she had so caringly knitted and given to me. We smoked, chanted and danced beauty back into our lives to the sound of the shaman's drum and rattle.

These exceptional teachings really helped me to get in touch with my inner core reality. I was being pushed to look inwards; right inside my very being. Slowly but surely, I began bringing about positive changes in my life. I discovered the brilliant being that I truly was. I was a child of the universe. I grew stronger and calmer and began to see my place in the greater scheme of things. I felt very fortunate in having these wonderful opportunities to grow. I had many supportive friends who helped me through the dark times. Very definitely, the fragmented feelings that I had of myself were gently being re-integrated. I felt more complete by having walked this path of beauty, the path of the sacred Medicine Wheel.

23 Call of the Wise Woman

ONE DAY, a few weeks after my vision quest, I was taking our dog for a walk across the school field when I became aware of a presence. He was shining and all light and about my height. He was walking right alongside me and stayed for quite a while. Then he disappeared!

Later that day, I had a young friend who came to stay with me overnight. She stayed with us occasionally when we went to a weekly Tarot reading course in Bath. That evening, I started to feel quite feverish, but the strange thing was that I felt fine inside. It didn't feel at all like a normal fever. I went to bed early, leaving this friend to talk to Godfrey.

As I prepared for bed, I saw this same shining being standing behind the bedhead which backed onto a wall. The wall didn't seem to be a problem to him. I lay down and immediately started to doze off . . .

I find myself sitting around in a circle with a lot of others. There is a fire burning in the middle. As I focus, I am looking across the circle at a Native American man with brown trousers and a pale green bandana around his head. His hair hangs down, long. He is looking at me intently and without moving. Suddenly, there is a voice from somewhere in the circle, which challenges me and says that the medicine name that was given to me during the medicine wheel workshop was not correct. I would have to die now and be reborn, then be given a new name. That this is a purification fire. I am told to step into the fire. I am feeling somewhat surprised at this request and as I stand there it feels as if I am burning, yet at the same time not burning. It is most extraordinary. Then I am given a new name, 'Rainbow Waters'. Soon, I feel a cool breeze dancing around me, cooling me down. It is a most delicious experience, especially after the heat of the fire and I start to feel better.

The next thing I know is that I am watching the back of a girl with long black plaits. She is wearing rusty brown doe skins, wading up to her waist in the water of a beautiful lake. She seems to be pushing out a raft. The next moment, I discover that it is actually me lying on this raft and this is why I am feeling the cool air around me. Then the scene ends and my 'fever' seems to disappear.

The next day, I felt as if I was not quite back in my body, but I still went to the tarot class. As I walked into the room for the session, the teacher 'saw' a Navajo Indian walking in beside me! She told me he was my guide.

I felt as if I had been given a new body. I felt different somehow...

Later, I worked with some other teachers who ran magical groups, exploring spirituality through Celtic magic. I participated in a long weekend course on Women's Mysteries. Eventually, I was initiated to the ancient magical tradition of the Mother Goddess in all her aspects.

I felt that as women, we needed to get more in touch with that divine feminine which is in us all. Women around the world had been second class citizens for far too long. We needed to rediscover our own personal power. I also felt that we needed to somehow redress the balance . . .

'The Eternal Mother . . . She, the great life impulse, always activating the seed, encouraging the urge to grow . . . Who is with ever open arms ready to welcome back the faltering spirit.'

For a while, I was fairly contented and happy with the group of people I found myself with. I was taking control of my own life and I was assuming my own personal integrity. It felt like I had reached another level in understanding myself. I felt clean and clear. More complete. The teachings that I had received were excellent and now I felt that I could move on in my life free of past demons and negative thought patterns.

I set up a group for women and we met regularly in each other's houses, participating in various healing circles and together we studied the ancient mysteries. We went out frequently to celebrate some festival or other in various sacred sites and this fed my sense of adventure and mystery. I was curious to learn about the nature of the elements and how they were the 'building blocks' of the very fabric of the universe. These elements were all around me in every shape and form, solid or otherwise. Once, I 'stirred up' an element...

One evening, we did a special ceremony in our lounge. It was held at a very auspicious time. We cast the circle. Everyone was silent. The energy was electric and all of us were very focused. I started the group with a creative visualization meditation, which helped with our given intention as a group.

We wrote down all the things we wished to clear away from our lives. All our old, bad habits and negative thought patterns and anything that was not valid any more. Then, I placed a small candle in a pot on a brass tray and put it in the centre of our circle. We started by chanting and sending our own personal negativities into this pot . . . Suddenly, there was a spark and the whole thing caught fire. The wax from the small candle had melted and overflowed into hot liquid flames in the pot and spread all over the tray. Without thinking, I quickly picked up the whole lot, broke the circle and ran out carrying the flaming offering into the garden where I chucked some earth on the top of it as fast as I could. I quickly cleaned out the vessel, replaced the candle and placed it all back on the tray, then re-entered the circle. We continued with the ritual as if nothing had happened.

It transpired that a fire elemental had 'attached' itself to me and remained with me for a good three months. I could set fire to wet matches and, if I stood near a lighted candle, it would start to flare up and spit. I could make the dying embers of a fire become a raging blaze. I had never had such an effect on fire before. Godfrey and I were invited to a New Year's Eve party in Wales. It was the place where I had done my first vision quest. I stood by the bonfire which was well ablaze because it was a cold night. It immediately started to sizzle and burn more rapidly the moment I moved near it, then — it suddenly stopped! The fire elemental simply disappeared back into the fire never to return.

New things started to happen to me. I had always been able to 'sense' other energies around. I found that I could see people's auras. I didn't know what the colours and shimmering lights meant, but I could see them. At other times, especially with the backdrop of darkness, I began to 'see' different situations as if they might have been past life experiences. They came to me particularly when I was resting or just before dropping off to sleep. Suddenly, there would be a shift in my consciousness and I would be aware of a change of circumstances around me and find myself in another reality which was sometimes rather disconcerting. Then I would find myself back in my bed or wherever I was sitting before the vision occurred. In our group, we would discuss all these phenomena. Others in the group had also experienced many interesting things and we enjoyed sharing them. After a time, I became tired of these discussions as they weren't really getting me anywhere. I had understood how they happened, and why, and they were all very interesting, but . . .

A new kind of restlessness entered my heart. With all the glimpses and experiences I had had, the effects always seemed to wear off after some time. Truth, I felt, could not just come and go as it pleased. I sensed that truth was eternal, and that which was eternal never changed. How could I tap into that state and remain in it all the time? I just knew there had to be more than all these temporary glimpses. It is true, that I had had some amazing experiences along the way, but, so what?

Leaving no stone unturned, I continued my search everywhere for the definitive truth. I was hungry and empty.

cleansing the vessel

"...We search for Paradise
But all we find is a
Handful of dust
Is this the end?
Nay, my friend
Love bonds the hearts
And heals us now
To trust – oh to trust
A memory of
Long ago..."

(Poems from My Heart, 'My Spirit Soars')

24 who am i ?

IN THE EARLY 90's, I made an interesting discovery. I was browsing in a bookshop one day and a little book caught my attention. It was called *Be As You Are* and it just seemed to fall off the bookshelf and into my hands. I had fallen in love with the title. It was full of questions and answers based on the teachings of Bhagavan Sri Ramana Maharshi and edited by David Godman. Ramana Maharshi was a sage who had lived and died at the foot of a very sacred mountain, called 'Arunachala', in South India. These teachings were profound and stirred an ancient feeling, an ancient knowing deep, deep inside me. This book contained a simple message and really spoke to me. This was Truth with a capital T! Ramana Maharshi said that all the questions that anyone ever asked, could be answered by simply asking ourselves . . . 'Who am I?' Was it really that simple? I thought. I was so excited. Each word seemed to speak to some part of me and I wondered how one went about actually having the deep and meaningful experience it talked about.

I thought of my old friend with the beard. He once said to me . . . 'and tell me, who is it that says that, anyway?'

Another process had started to happen within me. Silently and subtly, something was stirring deep in my heart. Reading this book, I had unwittingly touched on the Truth. This was it. Here was the answer to all of my questions. But how could I really begin to experience it?

A gentle voice started to speak quietly in the back of my mind. 'When the ego is gone . . .'

That was it. Yes. I need to let go of my ego self . . .

Then my old friend's voice came back like an echo of a similar idea. 'You know the ego is gone when you feel no welling-up inside you of pride, of personal feelings of the "I am doing" variety . . . Then, and only then, you really know that the ego is gone. You will know that you have understood your true essential nature, the source of all.

'Life cannot ever be the same again once this ego is gone . . . Listen to your listening . . .

'When the ego is gone, there is no possibility of slipping back inadvertently.

'In this very moment you can be free. You are already there . . .

'You just have not quite understood it yet . . .'

My old bearded friend from my childhood. He was reaching out to me from somewhere in the back of my mind. His voice continued...

'Do you remember the analogy of the still lake with the clouds reflected in it?'

'Yes, yes'. . . I remembered . . .

'Now, let your mind go still like the surface of the lake . . .

'With no attachment to all these thoughts.

'You know that "no attachment" means no dialogue, no discussion, no anxiety.

'Watch them come and go like clouds on the lake . . .

'Just go . . . quiet.

'Dive deep into this Source.

'Quiet without looking,

'Quiet without listening,

'Quiet without speaking,

'Quiet with silent detachment of the mind.

'Slip into stillness . . . merge . . .

'Silence teaches us to . . . just be who and what we have always been . . . Consciousness.'

Yes, this was it. My old friend was speaking the same truths that were presented in this book *Be As You Are*. Another old memory returned . . .

One day, a long time ago, my old bearded friend and I were standing on the top of Cooper's Hill not very far from where we lived. Every year, when I was small, there was a big cheese-rolling competition. They had great big Gloucestershire cheeses that people would chase. I don't remember what the winners won. Perhaps it was the huge cheese! It was quite an amazing event which we always watched.

On this particular occasion, there was no cheese-rolling event, but just a sunny morning with nobody else around. Just the two of us . . .

I said, 'What if I was to see that I really am consciousness, right now, right at this very moment? I mean can *consciousness*, which is me, really *know* itself? And if so, how does it know itself? And is it true that I could be happy all the time if I really did know it?'

'Umm,' he winked. 'Yes, always, because you will have discovered where the source of all true happiness lies.' He continued . . . 'you will live in a spontaneous way, light and free. You will be awake to being awake.'

'Be awake to being awake? What do you mean?' I asked.

He smiled, 'When you wake up to the fact that that which gives you true inner happiness, **is** about being NOW. To be in the NOW, we have to be very spontaneous. Right **now**, and in this very moment. Not a minute ago or in a minute's time. That is how you can be awake to being awake.'

For a long time, I thought and meditated on this truth and I finally came to some conclusions . . . That when I live very consciously and with awareness of this present moment, I am able to be spontaneous. That is, I can live a little more in the 'now,' right in this very second. By being spontaneous, I was being invited to live more fully, more freely. The invitation began to feel rather like being given a winning lottery ticket. I just needed to experiment. Here was an excuse for me to do some things I had not allowed myself to do before. Did I need an excuse? I would have to dare to take a few risks. Spontaneity was a gift to myself!

To be truly spontaneous, I would have to look at and drop all the baggage of old patterns of behaviour that I was carrying around with me as it was too heavy for this kind of game. Here was a wonderful opportunity for me to wake up into this present moment. I could then be who I really am.

In *Be As You Are*, Ramana Maharshi said that our mind was 'just a bundle of thoughts'. So could I allow my ego to think that it thought of being spontaneous, all by itself? Could I 'con' my mind into thinking such a thing? I asked myself. My ego seemed to like being spontaneous . . .

It was by thinking in this way that I began to discover that there was actually a state of ego-less-ness about how I viewed everything. Yes, it was as simple as that.

I thought often about my dear old friend of my childhood days. He had given me such a rare gift. The gift of his time and his wise words that I was only now beginning to recognise and understand. I thought back to a time when I was sitting on the lawn at home listening to my friend. He was talking to me about my ego, otherwise known as my 'I'.

'Yes, my dearest child,' he said, 'we get very confused about this little ego of ours. This "I" is our ego personality.'

I asked, 'But where does the "I" come from?'

He continued, 'It all comes from our mind. The place where all our thoughts come from. Everything, and I mean absolutely everything that we can ever possibly think of, that exists in this world around us, comes from our minds. This includes our "I". This little personality of you and me. Do you remember once I said that our mind is made up of just a bundle of thoughts?'

Yes, I thought to myself, I remembered how I had been impressed by that thought . . . Ramana Maharshi was saying exactly the same thing.

He continued, 'And that "I" thought is the very first thought that comes to us, then all other thoughts follow it. This first thought is the root of all other thoughts.'

Then he said something that had completely baffled me at the time. *'If we look very carefully we will discover that our little "I" has never really existed. Why? Because we have confused this little personal "I" with that greater "I", which is at once within and without. Above and below. That greater "I" is that which transcends the root thought "I".'*

What had he meant by that? I had thought to myself. Ummm. . .

I began to wonder if I needed a teacher who could explain all this to me . . .

JUST ABOVE where we lived, there was a small Tibetan Buddhist centre. I went with a couple of friends to visit it one day and, to my surprise, a young woman who had been in our women's magical group was sitting in the *gompa* (meditation room). She had become interested in Buddhism and had joined this community. I enquired into what was going on there. I decided to go along to some of the meetings and learn more about Buddhism.

I joined some of their classes and studied some of the holy Buddhist texts and attended some pujas. These were special ceremonies to develop specific aspects within ourselves. We did different pujas to honour and to connect with the different Buddhas. All these teachings were designed to help us to change and purify our minds. To help us to become more caring, loving human beings and to develop true Buddha-nature within ourselves. I came to understand that this 'Buddha-nature' was the same thing as the 'Self' that Ramana Maharshi talked about.

Our teacher was an ordained nun who ran and taught at this centre and was one of many teachers who taught this tradition around the world. She was very clear in her teaching, which impressed Godfrey who soon became interested too.

I decided to go to the Spring Festival which was held in Cumbria. I was keen to see the Tibetan Lama, known to his disciples as Geshe-La, who was the principal teacher and spiritual guide. I sat as near to the front as possible so that I could get a real sense of who he was. I was greatly impressed. As I sat quietly listening to what he was saying, I became aware of a light emanating and dancing all around his body. I felt that I was in the presence of a real, 'enlightened' being. Here was a living Buddha showing us all how we could discover our true nature. I was really happy to have met such a pure teacher as this Lama.

One day, I took part in a retreat on the tantric practice of Vajrayogini. During the meditation, I slipped into that very still inner place and found myself sitting on a high hill in the sunshine. I became aware of the presence of Geshe-la who had come and sat down beside me. I looked up at him and saw that his eyes were looking in opposite directions in a sort of 'wall-eyed' way and I 'knew' in that instant that he was omniscient. He could see in all directions! Then his eyes became normal. He smiled, then put his arm around me and pointed far into the horizon. I looked and saw a vast desert with a beautiful shining city right in the centre. Light was emanating from this city.

He then spoke and said, 'If you work hard, you will attain this.' Wow . . . A Pure land . . . It was a most beautiful and inspiring moment . . .

Over the course of time, I received many empowerments. I went to California in order to receive the Medicine Buddha and Green Tara empowerments as well as the Pawa practice from Geshe-La. I loved the Green Tara pujas. These pujas really connected me with the power and majesty of Tara. Tara is a female Buddha, who is swift to help all those who call to her in their distress and she never lets anybody down as I soon discovered.

I made a strong connection with Green Tara through a very interesting experience. She had a profound effect on me . . . I had lost my glasses and I couldn't find them anywhere. We were due to meet a very important Lama who was visiting the Centre from India. Time was short and I was agitated. I quickly sat down and meditated. I implored Tara to help me find them. I was focusing on her in my mind's eye. She was in the form of a statue when, all of a sudden, the image seemed to take on an energy of its own and a very beautiful being emerged. As she moved towards me she grew taller and taller. The moment she merged right into me, I suddenly found that I could *see* where the glasses had gone. They had fallen down underneath the passenger seat in my car. What a surprise I had when I went out to the car and found them there! Since that first experience, she has helped me many times.

The Medicine Buddha empowerment was very powerful. I felt connected to the beautiful healing energy. My teacher gave a profound explanation of how the Medicine Buddha could help us all in our lives. I was to appreciate how beneficial this empowerment would be for me in the years to come, especially when I took further steps to enhance my healing capacities and became a Reiki master, given that the founder of Reiki was also a practising Buddhist who loved the Medicine Buddha.

Whilst in California, I was privileged to have a personal audience with my Buddhist teacher. Then, just as I was about to leave, he hugged me. For the next few days I saw nothing but brilliant colours. Colours were everywhere I looked. It was like being in a Pure Land, in Heaven. Everything appeared bright and wondrous. I was in a daze, quite literally. At the same time, I felt a tremendous lightness of being as if I was walking two feet above the ground. I felt full of light wherever I went and that everything around me was also shining.

Where we were staying in Santa Barbara, I discovered a little bookshop not far away. It was attached to the Ramakrishna Vedanta Convent. I made friends with one of the nuns there who ran the bookshop. She was a real inspiration and helped me in so many ways to make my visit pleasurable. We had some very meaningful discussions on the spiritual life of the heart.

During one of my visits to the bookshop, I picked up a book on Dzogchen (Tibetan teachings on the Primordial, or non-duality). Now, this word 'Dzogchen' rang a bell. I thought of my dancing friend whom I had met in Delhi whilst studying Indian classical dance. I bought the book. Once again, it seemed that this truth was staring me in the face—yet I still had not fully understood it. The gods seemed to be teasing me. I already had a teacher who could explain the sutra and tantra teachings and I did so love these aspects of Buddhism, but what I really wanted, was to *be* the Buddha.

Once, I had a dream. I was standing in the gardens of Manjushri Buddhist Centre with Losang, a senior monk of Geshe-La. I was surprised to see that he was the same English monk that we had seen some ten years before in Mussoorie. Losang was explaining how we could understand the underlying reality of all things. In the dream, he called it 'the profound view of emptiness . . .' As he was explaining this to me, he moved his arm and hand very slowly and gently through the air.

Suddenly, I understood the meaning of the Buddha's teaching in the *Prajnaparamitra Sutra*:
'Form is Emptiness. Emptiness is Form'.

AFTER FOUR YEARS, we decided to sell our little home in mid-Wales as we didn't get to stay there as much as we had hoped. We began to look for a place nearer to Bath. Glastonbury was only fifty minutes' drive away and so we looked in that direction. I really liked Glastonbury and had visited it on a number of occasions over the years. Recently, I had spent some time there with Celia, a friend whom I had met in Bath. She had been looking for a place to live in that area.

Glastonbury is a holy place of pilgrimage for some and a healing sanctuary for others. A mixture of the profound and the profane. (a paradoxical place). A kaleidoscope of colours where all the hopes and fears of humanity are to be found in microcosm. Everybody we met there was very welcoming and we soon made friends. We had found a delightful little detached cottage with a small garden not far from the town centre. It was perfect.

One day, some friends invited me to go on a trip to see Mother Meera in Germany. She gave darshan by looking into one's eyes and bringing down the 'paramatman' light. This is divine light from Source. We were due to leave from Stroud and when I first arrived at the house where we had arranged to meet, there was a picture of Mother Meera on the refrigerator.

As I sat drinking a cup of coffee, it seemed that her eyes were smiling at me. Someone said that it often happened with that picture and that it was auspicious. We travelled together in a mini-bus, driving through Belgium, Holland and then towards Thalheim in Germany where Mother Meera lived. We stayed with a very hospitable German family who lived near a forest surrounded by beautiful countryside. It was about an hour and a half's drive from Thalheim.

The first night of the trip, I had a strange experience. I could not sleep very well. I went to the bathroom and on my way back to the bedroom there were two lightning flashes and when I got into bed there was a third one. There was no sound of thunder or rain. It was most peculiar. I lay down for a while and then I experienced a hot white flash of light shooting up through the left sole of my foot and right through my body. I felt full of light.

The visit to Mother Meera was amazing. She is very beautiful and I had a most powerful experience when she gave me her darshan. Her hands seemed huge on my head and again there was so much light. I felt 'connected' to a mighty source. When she looked at me, it was as if she swallowed me up in light. I could have stayed at her feet for ever just bathing in that luminosity.

About half-way through this visit, I had a waking dream. I was embracing Mother Meera then I went up in flames . . . I felt as if so much of my inherent sadness and difficulties were being burnt up. Soon after this, Godfrey and I celebrated our twenty-fifth wedding anniversary with a very beautiful ceremony in our lounge. Thirty people came, whom we had known during our married life. We invited two very special friends to give the blessings. Nancy, our Baha'i friend, and Celia, a priestess of Isis. As I had just returned from Mother Meera, I decided to telephone and ask her if she would send a blessing for the ceremony on our special day.

During the ceremony, the sun came out and shone brilliantly through the windows. The room was unusually full of light for late February. Many photos were taken and each picture had shafts of light shining across the room, filling it with radiance. Everything that was reflected in the room seemed more brilliant than ever and I knew that Mother Meera had sent her darshan to us. Everybody felt blessed. Afterwards, we went to Lyme Regis together for a little break away. Everyone waved us off—just like a newly married couple!

Before our move to Glastonbury, I had visited a very talented palmist who lived there. I had decided to go for a reading. It proved to be a very interesting session. I was impressed and told Godfrey about him and so he also decided to go for a reading. It was interesting seeing how our separate readings overlapped. We were obviously made for each other!

Whilst we were in Lyme Regis having our lunch, we heard a familiar voice at a neighbouring table which turned out to be our palmist friend who was also having his lunch. We all sat together and had a good chat. We arranged to have another 'reading'. This reading was to be a very interesting one, in that he 'foretold' that something 'big' would happen to me in my fifty-fourth year. I was intrigued . . .

27 being together

GODFREY AND I didn't see much of each other during the nine years he was working at the school. The weekdays were always busy and most weekends, he was out coaching boys rowing or taking them to regattas in different parts of the country. I missed him a lot and as I was not involved much in the life of the school, I tended to stay most of the time in Glastonbury with Charlie where we played music or practiced qigong which we were both fond of doing.

Fortunately, the opportunity to take early retirement came Godfrey's way and he decided to take it as he could see that the ever increasing commitment to his job was undermining the many interests that we held in common. This was a big one for Godfrey and he thought seriously about the consequences of stopping work. He had been a devoted teacher for many years but now, he agreed, was the time to make our life together more meaningful. We were excited by this prospect but nothing was clear to us at this point.

We took the opportunity to go travelling. Our first port of call was to visit our friends Praveen and Myrna, Charlie's old teacher in India. They were now retired and living in North Carolina. It was a joy to reconnect with these old friends. We had so much to share and talk about. It had been quite a few years since we had last seen them. They were now immersed in a meditative life and enjoyed living simply. Their example inspired us to see what was important in life.

As a treat, they took us to stay for a couple of nights at the Meher Baba ashram, situated at Myrtle Beach, South Carolina. It was a very peaceful and beautiful spot and just a turning off what our friends called 'glitz strip'. It was strange leaving a world of casinos and hotels for acres of virgin forest. Of course, when Meher Baba had stayed there, the whole area had been covered by forest but 'progress' in the form of places for entertainment had gradually encroached over the ensuing years.

They had felt that the atmosphere was the closest to India that could be found in that part of America. They had booked us all into a delightful log cabin bordering a very beautiful lake. The next day, we went out in a little rowing boat. The lake was rumoured to have alligators in it, but fortunately for us, they didn't seem too hungry and we only made 'sightings' of what we thought *might* have been alligators, although they could have just been logs.

From North Carolina we flew to Toronto to see my sister and brother-in-law, Yvonne and Paul. It had been snowing and was bitterly cold but I was really excited to see the snow. We had a great time exchanging our news as so much had happened to us all since we'd last been together. We walked a lot and took their dogs down some good trails not far from their house.

One day, they took us on a trip to a Chinese Buddhist temple in downtown Toronto. It had two large stone snow-lions sitting on each side of the entrance. There was also a very beautiful statue of Kwan Yin, the Goddess of Compassion, holding a baby, outside in the courtyard, whilst in the large temple there was a huge reclining Buddha. The devotees inside the temple were mainly Japanese and were very helpful in answering any questions.

On our travels we had thought a lot about whether or not to move. We were happy in our house in Glastonbury. It was spacious and well designed. The front of it faced westwards overlooking some common land where people walked their dogs. The views extended towards the Somerset Levels and we had the feeling of being in the heart of the country, yet in the town at the same time. The sunsets were particularly glorious.

Returning from our travels, we discovered that a builder had bought the common land opposite and was proceeding to build twenty-three houses on it. We were stunned as we would now lose our view of the beautiful countryside and those sunsets . . . That decided it. It was definitely time to move.

The three of us agreed that it might help in our decision-making as to what to do with the rest of our lives, if we went and spent some time at the Amitabha Buddhist Centre, which was situated in beautiful grounds in West Quantoxhead, near Minehead between the Quantocks and the Bristol Channel. We rented out our house for three months to a young couple we knew and went to live in a large bed-sitting room with just a few of our belongings and our three animals. We also took 'Shirley', our camper van, which we kept just below our window. Charlie had his own room elsewhere in the Centre.

The community was made up of experienced practitioners including a number of nuns and monks, who formed the nucleus; a few young families with children; some mature adults with the odd dog and cat as well as a variety of non-Buddhist residents. There were also young people who came and worked as volunteers around the house and grounds. It was therefore quite a large community and we all took turns helping in the kitchen, cooking and washing up. It was a challenge to provide food for the sixty or so residents.

In the Gompa (meditation room), one of the things I enjoyed doing was setting out an offering of a hundred water bowls on a side table, which meant taking them down late at night in the traditional way. It was a meditation in itself, requiring focus and concentration as there were several special mantras to repeat at the same time as filling the bowls with water. To experience such beautiful moments was wonderful and a great privilege.

I was happy that we had decided to spend some time there. It gave us the opportunity for time out to think and also to deepen ourselves in the Buddhist teachings. We had many discussions, exploring the realms of immortality and about how we could eventually become released from the cycle of samsara. We participated in the many practices which were on offer as well as embarking on one of the major study programmes. I was keen to learn how to empty my mind which was full of rubbish and irrelevant thoughts most of the time. Thoughts that were detrimental to me. Could it be possible to empty one's mind so totally that truth could enter in? Was this the way forward? I knew that we had the choice to change our minds, but we didn't always recognize that possibility and it certainly wasn't always easy to do. I had not yet discovered the trick.

From the Buddhist Centre, I often walked down to the sea. There was a lovely walkway through several fields and past a large caravan park, which led down to the pebbled beach and old coal wharf. Many interesting fossils were to be found there. It was an interesting and invigorating place to visit and the dogs enjoyed a good walk. On one of these trips, I was feeling pretty contented. The sun was shining and it was warm. Suddenly, I became aware of some presences near me and then I saw the most amazing sight. There were four beings floating in front just above my head. They looked just like Buddha beings in a sitting position and they were all smiling at me. They seemed to be made out of extremely brilliant light which emitted many different colours dancing all about them.

Predominantly, there were various pastel shades of greens, pinks, blues and yellows. My heart felt really open and powerful feelings of love started to pour down from these beings into me. I was overwhelmed by the amount of love and compassion that emanated from them. Peace enveloped me. I noted that this sensation which had entered into my consciousness was the very essence of that peace for which I was searching.

There was a great similarity in the experiences that I had had over the years, searching in my heart, meditating, contemplating and diving deep into the very core of my being. So many things had happened to me during this search for truth. I was blessed and had always felt supported by these unseen forces. Something greater than myself was impelling me to continue this journey.

Generally, life was interesting and nourishing. I enjoyed many aspects of the community and it was always helpful having like-minded people around (Sangha). I learned so much through discussion. We were encouraged to spend time memorising the various books and texts. This proved difficult for me. However, I had no difficulty remembering the essence of the teachings, which I felt was more important, especially as I was wanting to empty my mind. I wasn't interested in becoming a Buddhist scholar.

After three months Godfrey and I moved back to our home in Glastonbury. Charlie loved being in the Centre and stayed on.

We planned the next step of our new life together . . .

AFTER A LOT of deliberation, we decided to go to France and see if we could find a property suitable for setting up a spiritual centre of our own. Godfrey was familiar with the French lifestyle having spent a lot of his youth there. He was a fluent French speaker. My language skills would have to be developed, having only studied French for a year or so in Canada. Our friend, Celia decided to join us on this initial trip. She felt a strong connection with France. We travelled in 'Shirley' right through the French countryside visiting many beautiful villages and towns. We stopped in several places that looked interesting along the way. The sun got steadily warmer as we approached the Loire Valley. There were so many beautiful spots to choose from, but none of them really 'spoke' to us.

Eventually, we found ourselves in the South-West of France where there were the remains of ancient Cathar castles perched on top of very high and craggy cliffs. The scenery was stunning. Brilliantly coloured geraniums decorated the windows and the gardens of nearly every house in the little villages and the fields were full of sunflowers which were growing just about everywhere.

The sun was very hot by the time we reached a great place to camp at 'La Pause' just outside Rennes-les-

Bains. It was beautiful, but extremely humid. We spent a lot of time just standing in the cool waters of a little rock pool nearby, surrounded by thick trees and bushes which created a cool, green, and magical environment. Dragonflies danced all around us.

We finally ended our search in the Quercy region— an interesting and hilly area situated between Cahors and Toulouse where the climate was more gentle.

We set about looking for the perfect place and stopped in the town of Caussade where, for the first time, we saw properties in an estate agent's window which not only looked as if they were possibilities but were also well within our budget. On the very last day of our trip, we were taken to see an old farmhouse which was virtually in ruins set in ten acres of beautiful park and woodland. We all agreed that this was a great find. We thought that people would like to come and stay in this beautiful, spacious and peaceful setting. It certainly seemed to be a place conducive to meditation and contemplation. 'Linon Haut', the name of the farmhouse, was just outside the medieval village of Montpezat de Quercy. It sat on the top of a hill overlooking a beautiful valley. The Pyrenees could be seen on particularly clear days, usually when it was going to rain! We decided there and then to buy the place. We were very excited, and having set in motion the preliminaries for the purchase, we drove back across France to catch the car-ferry to England.

Three months later, we returned to 'Linon Haut' towing a caravan. This was to be our 'home' once we began the renovations. The driveway to this property was almost a mile long and the fields on each side of the track were filled with thousands of sunflowers. They were magnificent. We unhitched the caravan and parked it under some trees in the woodland. This woodland area was also home for lots of birds. Many different kinds of wild orchids were growing all over the land and each variety was stunningly beautiful. There were quite a few mature fig trees in the garden and close to the house.

Soon after our arrival we were conscious of little furry beings scurrying between the walls of the house and the fig trees along the electric cable. These animals turned out to be 'loirs' or edible door-mice who seemed to be very active, especially in the middle of the night. They had large, round eyes like bush babies and tails like squirrels. They were very cute but turned out to be the principal agents of destruction to the fabric of the house.

The renovation of this old farmhouse was going to be a major undertaking as there were no interconnecting doors, or windows. Most of the floor boards were rotten and there were gaping holes everywhere. It was a big project and we would need to find the right people to help turn it into a habitable place. This would take time as we knew nobody.

One day, a lady wandered up onto our site with her grand-daughter and during our conversation we discovered that several of her relatives happened to be builders in the area. What luck! We both felt that she had been 'sent' to help us out.

Soon Gilbert arrived. He was typically French, built like a tank and constantly sporting the chewed end of a Gauloise-type roll-up which drooped miraculously from his lower lip. He turned out to be a great builder and stone mason and became a good friend. He was very excited about the project and agreed to start work almost immediately. He worked hard, devoting all his time to the re-creation of our new home. The two-foot thick walls of the house were soon full of more holes as he bashed his way through them, making spaces for doors and windows where before there had been none. Downstairs had been used for farm animals and a couple of mangers were still in position. Upstairs, was where the old owners had slept some twenty years prior to our arrival. There were no toilets. With the renovations well underway, dust was in the very air we breathed and we were eating grit most of the time.

Several friends came out to visit us and generally helped about the place. Visitors were always good for morale! Everybody loved 'Linon Haut' and could see its potential. Nicolas came and stayed for three months, helping with the building work and earning money as a local fruit picker. We all had a lot of laughs together and the weather was superb. We ate most of our meals outside under a parasol looking at the beautiful view of countryside with its occasional glimpses of the distant Pyrenees.

As we began to settle in to our new life, we met a lot of interesting people and I had to work hard at learning French. Godfrey was in his element, speaking to just about everyone he met and he loved cycling out on one of the old bikes to the village bakery each morning to buy fresh *croissants* and *pains au chocolat* for breakfast.

Early one morning, a large deer with magnificent antlers came wandering out of the woods towards me as I was sitting meditating on the garden swing seat. He stood absolutely still, staring at me. It was a beautiful shared moment until Kizzy, who was sitting beside me, started barking as she picked up the scent of this intruder. He was gone in a flash.

Occasionally, we saw what appeared to be mini crop circles in the long grass near the entrance to our land but we were told that the flattened grass was caused by wild boar who obviously enjoyed a jolly good roll. Unfortunately, we never actually saw one.

Next door to us, there was a 'bio-dynamic' vineyard. This meant that the vines were being planted and pruned by the phases of the moon and no chemicals were added to the wine. How lucky we were. Over the time, Denis the owner and his son provided us with endless supplies of delicious organic red wine. Denis was pretty healthy and was nearly a hundred when he died so it can't have done him too much harm!

After months of caravan living, we moved into the house little by little and as each room became more and more habitable, we spread ourselves out. We were still eating grit and getting very cold as winter drew in. Quercy winters are freezing. I had been under the misconception that the South-West of France was always sunny and hot. It isn't true! It was a pretty hard winter for us. By the next summer though, we had created a very fine five-bedroomed house. 'Linon Haut' was truly magnificent.

We had spent a good six months renovating it and now we needed to focus on setting up the place ready to receive guests. But unfortunately, funds were running out.

IN THE midst of our struggles in France, my sister wrote to me saying that she was going to see Usharbudh Arya. She had met him again after all these years whilst he was on one of his round-the-world teaching tours. He was due to give a lecture on Yoga Meditation in downtown Toronto. She had seen it advertised and so went to meet him. I thought that it would be nice for me to get back in touch with him again. It had been many years since I'd had last seen him.

I decided to write to Usharbudh. He was residing in India. He wrote back pretty quickly and was really pleased to hear from me, inviting me to go and visit him. He had become Swami Veda Bharati and was now the Spiritual Director of the Sadhana Mandir Ashram in Rishikesh, which had been established by the well known guru, Swami Rama of the Himalayas. I had had enough of eating grit and shivering in the freezing cold and so there and then I decided to go and visit him in Rishikesh. Godfrey was really supportive and thought that it would be a wonderful opportunity. Who knew where it all might lead?

So I packed my bags and invited Charlie, a keen yoga practitioner, to come with me. He was excited at the prospect of a trip to India and he quickly re-arranged his life for the next month. We met at the

Indian High Commission in London where we got our visas and, after great difficulty, we managed to obtain some tickets to fly a day later. We spent the night with some kind friends in Hampstead, then off we flew to spend a month in search of Truth.

We were met at New Delhi airport by one of the ashram taxis that had been sent down to collect us and we finally arrived in Rishikesh in the middle of the night, very excited. Charlie and I were given a sweet little room in the heart of the ashram.

The ashram is situated beside the sacred Ganga. It is a paradise, dominated by the majestic Himalayas whose eternal glory lies reflected in the beautiful waters of the holy Ganga. The sky was an intense and clear blue. The ashram and its gardens were truly peaceful and the people who lived and worked there were friendly and welcoming.

I could hardly wait to meet Usharbudh again after some forty-two years. We may have been physically separated, but on another level it felt as if we had never really parted. I was sitting in the yoga meditation hall when he came in to take the morning session. We instantly recognized each other and smiled. His love was pouring out to us as we sat there quietly. Later, we met and talked. Usharbudh (Swamiji) was so pleased to see me again and to meet Charlie. I knew that destiny had re-connected us.

Unbeknown to us, it was the International Yoga Week in Rishikesh. Everywhere we went was bustling with people who had come for this event from all over the world. Yoga classes were given daily at the ashram by visiting teachers and also by the resident teacher. Various lectures were given on different aspects related to yoga practice, including Ayurvedic medicine.

I frequently walked by the Ganga and just sat there. It was heaven. It was so good to be back in India after such a long time. I began to unclutter my head and to unwind slowly, stretching my body in the yoga classes and my mind in the meditation sessions. I started to breathe. I wanted peace and clarity. Here, I felt nourished. Swamiji was nurturing and breathing new life into me. Charlie and I spent some beautiful moments together, sharing various thoughts and ideas. We were both intoxicated by the heavenly atmosphere around us. Swamiji and I spent time reminiscing about the Gloucestershire days and how he had so loved coming to our home. Now I was being given a most beautiful welcome in his home and in his heart. Sometimes, I would go and sit in the room next to Swamiji, meditating in his presence without him knowing. Maybe he did know. I could feel his loving peacefulness coming through the walls. This was what I needed. Space to think and to just be.

One incident happened during this trip which was to be a great lesson in surrender. When we had flown into New Delhi airport, I had just three hundred rupees which I had kept from the time when we had been living in India. The airport bank was shut but there was a little table with a man sitting behind it, where money could be exchanged. However, the man could not give me any money with my visa card. Only cash for cash. Charlie, sensibly, had organised his money before leaving London. So, when we arrived, we had just enough money to pay for our taxi fare up to Rishikesh.

During the next few days, I explored the possibilities of accessing some money. No bank in Rishikesh or anywhere else within striking distance would accept my credit card and so there I was, stuck in India with only three hundred rupees! What to do? I began meditating in earnest and learned how to 'let go'. I was told that this was all I had to do . . . surrender. But it was not easy. My mind rebelled. I had to learn to trust that things would work out. Total faith was called for here. I had to surrender not only in my heart, but also in my head and as soon as I started to do that I discovered how the universe worked. Help and money began to arrive in the most unusual ways and eventually I was able to pay my way. We only have to trust, **really** trust, then our prayers will be answered. I had learned a big lesson.

During our stay at the ashram, both Charlie and I were initiated by Swamiji into the Himalayan Tradition of Yoga Meditation. He also initiated both of us into the Gayatri Mantra. We bathed in the sacred Ganga before the latter event and I thought about the millions of other pilgrims and seekers after truth who, over the centuries, had taken a purificatory bath in this sacred river. It was a poignant and beautiful moment: the water was so luminous and clear.

I wrote a poem . . .

By the River Ganga

Just as my mala

is washed

of all dirt

in the waters

of Mother Ganga,

may I also become

purified —

a shining jewel

to illuminate all worlds.

FIRE IN MY HEART

Sitting by you, Mother —

I regard you as the

External flow

of my

interior.

Water

regards

water.

O Shiva

You who radiate

from my crown

in all

the ten directions

Purifying

clarifying

emptying

cleansing

quickening

my Heart —

CLEANSING THE VESSEL

The Seat of

my Mind

Loving all beings

What would I be

without

Your constant care.

I am nothing

but what you make me

A servant for others.

O Gurudeva —

you are my Lord Shiva

In head and heart

to you I bow.

May my first thought

be a loving one

Make me a pure vessel

through which

the Divine Mother

may enter.

Swamiji gave me an Indian name, 'Nandini', which means 'she who brings joy'. I would try and live up to that ideal! I had now been given a focus for my meditations. I felt much lighter and clearer, not only in my mind but also in my heart. I talked to Swamiji about our hopes, plans and struggles in France. He was very sympathetic and when it was time for us to leave, he told me to go and teach as soon as I could. So, having had a month of spiritual nourishment in the ashram, we took our leave and slowly made our way back home: Charlie to the UK and me, back to France and Godfrey. Again, the same friends in Hampstead put us up for the night and gave us a hearty meal before we continued on our separate ways.

I ARRIVED back in Montpezat, the day of our 29th wedding anniversary and although I was pretty tired from the long journey, I mustered up the energy to go and celebrate with Godfrey in the local auberge.

It was good to be back home. Godfrey hadn't found it easy while I was away. The house and surrounding area looked like a bomb site and the grit was still everywhere. Yet, I was refreshed and my heart was gladdened. I was ready for the next stage, whatever that might be. I had been empowered by this trip. It felt as if a tremendous shift had happened within me. I needed to continue to nurture this feeling. Maybe teaching yoga would be the answer? I had been happy to reconnect with Swamiji after all these years. Now, the link was re-established and not just on the physical realm.

Once the lounge was more or less finished, I began to teach yoga and meditation in it. Our new lounge was a light and aïry space, and the sun's rays slanted through the windows for most of the day. I started morning sessions for a couple of 'early birds'. The early mornings were very chilly, so we lit the wood burner and made the room very cosy.

Over the years, I had learned a lot about the practice of yoga asanas (physical exercises) and was a keen meditator. I was familiar with the science of pranayama, the study of breath awareness—a process which helped quieten the mind more quickly, in preparation for meditation. So, now I started to learn how to teach yoga in French and had a small group of people who were interested in the classes. It wasn't easy teaching in another language to begin with, but most of the people were really understanding and we had a lot of fun and laughter together as I tried to explain things in my very questionable French.

Our life soon began to get a sort of a rhythm to it, which helped us settle down. I began to paint again. Inspired by my own meditations, I started painting Mandalas. Mandala designs just appeared out of the ether. They would manifest themselves in beautiful light forms right out of my consciousness and I shared them with my students in the formal meditation times. Many ideas for these Mandalas kept coming into my consciousness, so I painted and painted. I started teaching others how to paint them as a form of self-help. It became a tool for them too towards healing themselves and in this way discovering truth. At the same time, meditations just entered my mind and I wrote them down and used these with my students. People found them helpful and Godfrey kindly translated them all into French. Something magical was going on. I was sure that Swamiji was inspiring me.

In one of my many forays into the surrounding countryside, I found a little cave just big enough for me to sit in. Theoretically, it was just beyond our boundary, but as it was in the wilderness, I thought that nobody would mind too much if I used it as a place to meditate. It was situated off one of our tracks across some woodland and was beautifully quiet, with birdsong and the rustling of little creatures in the undergrowth. Here I found peace and stillness from the noisy building site.

The renovations continued and people came from all over the place to stay with us. Godfrey started to offer French classes to the ex-patriate community and had a few students from the UK coming over for 'A' Level revision sessions. We cooked all the meals. The food was all vegetarian and nobody seemed too bothered about not eating meat.

During the winter months Godfrey had to use the chain saw every day to chop wood for the two wood burners we had. He found it hard work and very time consuming. I lived in permanent fear of him injuring himself. A young couple of Australian 'woofers' (willing workers on organic farms) dropped by one day in their campervan and offered to help us around the place. They said that they could look after the grounds and trees and do all kinds of things including light building work. This sounded hopeful and so they stayed for five weeks. In exchange for work, we gave them food and board. They loved the land and were a great inspiration as they were so positive all the time, which helped to keep us going. One of them was a very talented musician and had played saxophone in the Australian Youth Orchestra and he often played my flute. Sometimes we played and drummed together.

As it was so hot, we spent most of the summer living and eating outside under the trees. It was very pleasant after the freeze of the winter. Life became easy.

Kizzy, our old dog, got ill. She had had problems with her breathing for some time. Eventually, it was clear that she was not going to last much longer. One morning, after her early morning outing, she came rushing back in on her own. She usually had to be carried in. She raced up the stairs (having jumped over a heavy guitar-case which we had placed across the stairway to stop her from coming up) and into our bedroom. She was panting heavily. I picked her up and she started to have a 'seizure' of some sort as she lay in

my arms. Probably due to her sudden exertion. She
was not at all well so I carried her downstairs and sat
with her in my arms for an hour or so. Then she went
very still and quietly died. I gently laid her back in her
basket and put my hand on her head for a while. I
could sense that her life-force was still in her body
although there was no movement.

She had had an interesting life and lived well for
fifteen and a half years. We covered her body and placed
it in a little box leaving it at the other end of the house.
She still needed time to leave her physical body before
we buried her. Later, we held a little ceremony for her
and our other two pets, Lizzi, another dachshund and
Muffy came and sat nearby. We buried her under a fig
tree, over which we had placed a large, stone Buddha.
Lizzi went right down into the hole to say her farewells.
Both animals seemed to understand what had
happened. It was very touching.

During this ceremony, I was to see a most amazing
sight. A small girl aged about two or three appeared
before me with very light ash blonde hair. I wondered
who she was. Kizzy's next incarnation perhaps?

31 attunement

CHARLIE CAME over to visit us for a month and brought his future wife, Katharina with him. They had met at a Buddhist festival. Charlie was very excited by the fact that they had been attuned as Reiki and Seichem Masters via the internet by an Australian couple. I was mildly surprised that an attunement could be done in that way. I was aware that it is quite possible for healers to send absent or distant healing to wherever it is needed so, after all, why not an attunement? Charlie had been impressed by them. I trusted his judgment, and I was also keen to receive the Master attunements. So I decided to write to them too and ask if they would attune me to Reiki Master, mentioning that Charlie was my son. They wrote back to say it was definitely possible and that they would be very pleased to give it.

I had received my Reiki1 attunement in Glastonbury, during which the great avatar Babaji had come into my consciousness as a helper. It had been a very powerful experience. I took my Reiki 2 attunement in France. The healing energy was consistently coming out of my right hand whenever I did a healing. It was very hot. I had always been interested in 'hands-on' healing since healing our cat.

In the meantime, Charlie gave me the Master attunement himself which I thought was really sweet.

It was to be a very powerful experience. A thin elderly Chinese man 'came through' in flowing robes, wearing a tall, old-style hat with flaps over the ears and he had a very long, wispy beard. He continued to help me whenever I gave healing sessions along with Babaji and a few 'others' who came through along the way.

After this attunement, the hot, healing energy was coming equally out of both of my hands. This was good. I felt more balanced. I wrote again to the Australian couple explaining what we had done. They were delighted with the result and also arranged for me to have the same attunement after which they would then issue me with a certificate of their own. They offered the attunement freely, as they felt that the Reiki energy should be made available to everybody and that it would help in the work that I was doing with my yoga. I was very touched by this and felt that they were really sincere, so the dates were set for the attunement.

Meanwhile, the renovating of the house had taken its toll on us in terms of money and energy. We realised very soon that we would have to increase our income substantially if we wanted to carry on living in France. It would then become necessary for us to join the French 'system' and pay the high social charges just as all the French do. After some enquiry, we found that it would be far too expensive for us and also a very long-winded business. So, with heavy hearts we abandoned our project and decided to return to the UK. We were disappointed that it hadn't worked out. Godfrey particularly so as he dearly loved France and had felt very much at home there. Although I loved the place where we lived, I had reservations about living and working permanently in France.

We packed up the house and made the trip to the UK via Belgium to Holland to stay for a night with Annemie, a very good Dutch friend whom we had first met whilst on a camping holiday in Vézélay in

Burgundy. She was keen to have Muffy as she had recently lost one of her cats. Tompoes, her surviving cat was lonesome. Cats don't like being shunted around from pillar to post and we knew that our existence was likely to be nomadic for the next little while.

My Reiki attunement from the Australians was due to take place during the week that we were travelling. I contacted them about this fact and was assured that it would not be a problem. We stopped and spent several nights in different places along the way. I woke up in the middle of three separate nights with heat pouring out of both of my hands in a very persistent way. I felt a sense of lightness at the same time and I guessed that I was being sent the attunements. These moments were very powerful energetically and I felt very clear. I received both the Reiki and Seichem Master attunements in this manner and was now convinced of the efficacy of distant healing.

When we finally reached Annemie in Holland, the two cats met. At first, they kept a healthy distance from each other but after a while Muffy seemed content to settle down with her new-found friend, and we felt happy in the knowledge that she would be loved and well cared for.

coming home

"Ineffable Radiance
I Am That
I Am
That glimpse of
Truth Immortal
In My Self
My mortality
Dissolves into
Timelessness
Forever in
Union with
You"

(Poems from My Heart, 'I Am That')

32 finding the key

NOW WE were back in the UK, we had to find somewhere to live and a friend who had a house set in the woods near the Amitabha Buddhist Centre invited us to stay. We lived with him for three weeks and had a great time sharing news and ideas. We enjoyed reconnecting with a few old friends from the Centre and having a few meals together. It provided us with a temporary haven while Godfrey scanned the papers for a suitable job.

September had arrived and the sun was sitting low on the horizon, shedding a beautiful range of exquisite colours across the Quantocks, especially at sunset. The evenings were drawing in gradually and there was just the hint of a chilly breeze in the air which warned us of the return of the wintry months. The leaves were beginning to take on the most beautiful shades of pinks, reds, yellows and golds. I loved these days near the sea, but we were never quite sure what the next day would bring . . .

Staying at the Buddhist Centre, there was a young woman who was a devotee of a South American teacher called Satyananda, who gave some kind of teachings through 'Satsang'. She was arranging a trip to go and listen to him near Malvern in Worcestershire. I enquired as to what kind of teachings he gave, and she said that he was giving similar teachings to those of Sri

Ramana Maharshi. I was immediately interested and decided to go. This teaching was about non-duality, which I now discovered was called 'Jnana' yoga. The yoga of true knowledge.

When the day came, we piled into several cars and off we went. It took a couple of hours to get there. We finally came to a small hall in a village just outside Malvern having travelled through some very beautiful countryside. About thirty or so people had gathered for this meeting. Not a bad crowd I thought, considering that the venue was in an out-of-the-way place. Satyananda was said to have had some kind of an 'awakening'. I was told that his teacher had been a disciple of Sri Poonja (Papaji), who in turn had been a disciple of Ramana Maharshi. We sat down and started listening to what was going on. The format of the gathering was in the style of questions and answers. People asked questions and then he responded. It was an interesting approach that I had not come across before. A few people started asking questions about 'who we are' and 'what we think we are.'

The dialogues were interesting. Two young women who had come from the Buddhist Centre started asking questions designed to steer the meeting towards their understanding of Buddhism. Soon, they monopolised the time with these questions and people started getting a bit restless. I noticed that I was getting a bit annoyed too, especially as we had come a long way to hear what Satyananda had to say. Then I decided to focus on what his responses were to all these questions. He was very patient and gradually I grew less angry and became more peaceful and relaxed. His responses to the questions were short, simple and clear.

Whilst sitting in this quiet state, something sort of 'clicked' in my head. All the anger and frustration which had arisen in me had now left and I found myself more peaceful and remained in this receptive state listening carefully. It was as if Sri Ramana Maharshi himself was whispering his extraordinary love to me. It felt like this teacher had become a clear channel whereby Ramana Maharshi could communicate directly to me.

The spoken words were suddenly becoming more like a gentle vibration that enveloped my very being, *experiencing* these words rather than conceptualising them. This was it. The understanding, the clarity that this vibration, whatever it was, was the light of my own divine nature, deeply rooted in my heart. I knew that this was the happiness for which everybody was looking. Sri Ramana Maharshi was communicating his simple teaching directly into my heart space. through this teacher. Were others experiencing a similar thing? What good fortune had led me to this? Here was Truth. It was staring me in the face. In fact it *is* my face . . . What a shock! I was transported into this space of Total Being; not doing, not searching—just being. Just like the Buddha in fact! How simple it was.

After this, life did not seem quite the same any more. Something very special had happened to me at that small gathering in Worcestershire. For the first time, I started to feel a gentle sort of connection with something much greater than I could ever have possibly imagined. I began to *'feel'* connected to the very fabric of life itself.

This was exactly what my old friend had pointed out to me all those years ago. I saw that there had been a constant thread running throughout my life. It had taken me so many years to recognise it. Many times I had forgotten about the dreams and experiences that I had had in my life as the world was perpetually wooing me away. I was always being encouraged and helped by so many kind and beautiful teachers. Why had I never noticed—until now?

I remembered a dream that had said as much, which I had not understood at the time. Now, it was obvious.

I am on a journey and I am driving a car full of people, in a convoy. I arrive at a garage. I get out. Then, at the same moment, I manage to lose the vehicle. I am hunting everywhere for it and cannot find It. Some men come and offer help and together we go and visit a clairvoyant they know. I then begin to 'dream' within this dream that the same thing is happening all over again. I lose the vehicle again, and again I cannot find it. I am looking everywhere for it and this time I am really desperate.

I go in search of the men who had helped me before, and again they take me to see the clairvoyant.

She says to me, 'Don't you remember what I said before?'

I reply, 'Yes, but I am still not sure.' I follow the men out who have offered to help me to find my vehicle yet again, but this time I lose sight of them. Then I wake up without having found either the car or the men.

Now I understood that I needed to pay more attention. It seemed that I had to be shown again and again until I really understood what truth actually looked like. This was yet another spiritual lesson.

An interesting thing occurred later which was to stop me from feeling angry ever again. Something had upset me and a strong response arose inside me. I decided to sit with this feeling and see where it had originated within my body. I felt the tension in my solar plexus and allowed it to build up to a crescendo of raw energy. This energy formed itself into a flaming bright orange fire ball with lots of purple, yellow and black in it. It was a solid, moving mass of energy. I excluded all the negative thoughts surrounding the anger as I held it inside my chest. It felt heavy, sticky and thick. I then went outside and concentrated strongly on bringing this fire ball of energy up into my throat area. With a hard breath, I exhaled it forcibly into the atmosphere in front of me. Instantly, I felt a great relief in my chest and throat areas and, to my astonishment, a large figure made of what looked like static electricity manifested itself. It resembled a very huge wrathful deity like one from the Buddhist pantheon. It cracked and shimmered about fifty feet in front of me for just a few moments then it dispersed and disappeared into thin air.

'So this is what my anger looked like,' I thought. How shocking! I then wondered if all of our thoughts, whether good, bad or indifferent appeared in a different dimension from our normal awareness without us realizing it. I wondered if these shapes appeared all the time in different forms, depending upon our personal psychological conditioning and understanding of the world. We do not normally see our thoughts, but how terrifying it would be if we could actually see them, given that we spend virtually all of our time 'thinking'. I imagined all the space around us full of everybody's thought forms. So, now I worked on developing the 'witness' aspect of my mind to see if I could notice the thought before it arrived in a more concrete form. Ummm, this would be a challenge.

33 ṣurrender

AFTER THREE weeks, we left our friend's house in West Quantoxhead and moved across to Glastonbury. The next little while was a period of temporary accommodation, staying with various kind friends for a fortnight or so at a time. Glastonbury was where I really wanted to be if I had to stay in the UK.

Nowhere else was quite the same. We knew a lot of people in Glastonbury. We were offered a house to rent from some friends who were off to Hawaii for a couple of months. This gave us time to breathe. Their house was in a great location on a hillside near the Tor and overlooking the Somerset Levels. Dorothy, who owned the house, had spent some time out in India at Sri Ramana Maharshi's ashram. I was delighted to see so many books about him on her bookshelves. I read about his exemplary life and, as I read, I felt very drawn to this Sage. With the meeting near Malvern and now this opportunity to read about Ramana, it felt as if he had been waiting for me.

We still owned the French house and we debated whether we should continue to be in France for half the year. It was certainly a lovely site in which to receive guests. But should we sell it and spend all our time in England? Meanwhile, Godfrey had seen an interesting job advertised for an educational consultant in London.

In a very short time, he was offered the post. He was pleased and looked forward to the new challenge ahead.

One of the issues that would have to be faced was where to live now that Godfrey was going to be working in London. We looked through the local newspapers and saw an advertisement for someone who liked animals to stay as a companion in their house out on the Somerset Levels. The lady was very friendly and her house was a converted barn. We had a good chat, the outcome of which was that although it wouldn't be right for us to move in with her, there was the possibility that she might be selling her small house in Glastonbury, which gave us food for thought.

In the meantime, Godfrey started work. The long commute into London and back was extremely tiring, so he arranged to stay with some friends during the week and come back at the weekends. I missed having him around.

Not far from Glastonbury Abbey there was a little house with a courtyard for sale. We made an offer and started the process of buying it. As life had been rather hectic, we hadn't thought much about the reality of actually living in this place and gradually I realised that we had rather rushed into the purchase. Fortunately, there were a few hold-ups with the house for which I was thankful as it gave me more time to think. I was already starting to get 'cold feet' about buying this particular place and decided to back out of the sale there and then! I rang Godfrey and told him that my gut feeling was not to go ahead on this property and that I had already rung the solicitors to stop the process. He was somewhat shocked and he asked me if I was aware of the consequences of this action. I replied that I certainly was. I was quite surprised at my certainty.

We only had a week left before our friends were due back from Hawaii, so we had to find somewhere else to live quickly. I felt instinctively that I had done the right thing and that life always has a way of sorting things out as they should be, as long as we allow them to happen.

A day or so later, I was taking the dog for a walk when a large blue van drove, by flashing its lights at me. Immediately, a head popped out of the window and someone waved. It was the kind lady who lived out on the Levels. She had recognised our dog as she passed by. She was on her way up to her other property with a painter to redecorate it and was somewhat agitated as she had just been let down by the person who had been going to rent the place. Now she needed a new tenant as quickly as possible. What a stroke of luck! Not that I thought that 'luck' had much to do with it. This was most definitely a gift. It was a one-bedroomed house with a small garden and a pond with some fish in it. There was ample parking space and it was in a quiet location above the town with lovely walks to the Tor. In short, it was ideal and we made arrangements to move in and rent it for a couple of months. I was so excited and rang to tell Godfrey who was as amazed as I was at how things had worked out. We liked living in this dear little house and made some good friends in the immediate neighbourhood.

From then on, strange 'coincidences' or 'synchronicities' were constantly presenting themselves. What seemed 'normal' to me was fast disappearing and all I had to go on with was 'trust' and 'letting go' of any preconceived ideas of what I thought should be happening.

Early one morning, I had a strange and interesting experience. We had had a really busy time and this particular night I had not slept very well and was feeling dreadful. My body was aching and my eyes felt as if they didn't belong to me. As I was lying there in the bed, suddenly His face was there before me. Sri

Ramana Maharshi! His eyes so full of love and compassion. As He smiled at me, a wave of light and bliss entered my whole being. All my aches and pains began to go. His face appeared a second time and the same thing happened. This time, all the aches vanished completely. An all-pervading light and energy gradually enveloped and embraced me. I felt His loving warm presence stay around me for quite a while. I felt supported and connected to this most beautiful Sage, who had died fifty or so years before. How amazing to think that it is possible to be touched by such a presence across the ether.

WE EVENTUALLY sold our home in France and found another house to buy in a fairly quiet location near the centre of Glastonbury, which had everything we needed including a garden and a garage. It had a conservatory which overlooked the back garden and an extra attic room with a large velux window set into the roof which made it a very light and airy space. We turned this room into our sanctuary and called it the 'Ashram'. It was a perfect spot for meditation. I began to sit here regularly. I set up a few early morning sessions with a friend who lived opposite and her children sometimes joined us for a shared breakfast. When Godfrey had time, he joined me in the Ashram. We enjoyed being together in the silence. It always seemed special. What a gift! I was there every morning and very soon a palpable presence of peace that defied definition started to become evident.

Up until now, my life had been propelled in a constant search for the truth. The journey to ultimate happiness. Every part of the journey had been relevant and necessary. My likes and dislikes, joys and sadnesses. They had all accompanied me along the way. I saw that everything, literally everything and everyone, was a teacher for me. Over the years, I had often visualized a special place in the centre of my heart. The place where I always went during my meditations. It was a very beautiful and peaceful place. Often my spiritual teachers and guides would be there too and I had many questions answered.

Apart from Bhagavan Sri Ramana Maharshi, who had had such a great impact on my life, the only other teacher that I had not met in the physical level who also would be found in this special place was the Dzogchen master, Namkhai Norbu. I had been so influenced by his teachings when I first came across them that I felt I had made a connection with him on another dimension. Chokyal Namkhai Norbu's teachings and the teachings of Ramana were one and the same: the teachings of non-duality, the primordial.

Everything that I had received from the teachers that I had had the privilege to meet was about to ripen in a most extraordinary, life-changing way. These teachings were a fire in my heart.

In the early morning of the May Bank Holiday 2001, Godfrey and I were sitting quietly up in the Ashram. The atmosphere was peaceful. I started thinking about love. I thought about the meanings of universal love and compassionate love. What 'unconditional' love could possibly be like and began to meditate on this imaginary state . . .

The next moment . . .

No more moments . . .

The transition into this state was smooth; instantaneous. There was no knowing at which point 'it' happened. The 'I' was meditating no longer. The mind had cut out. Floods of love and bliss emanated from the very core of my being. Light was extending in all directions. Light everywhere . . .

Wave upon wave of bliss and light pulsated continually through this body.

The totality of all there was, is and could ever be was in this instantaneous flash.

Total Unconditional Love.

Brilliant awareness overtook this small perspective of life . . . everything was crystal clear . . .

Suddenly my 'I-ness' was extraordinarily 'alive' to all that surrounded me and was in me . . .

The unity of all things. Pure Consciousness is all there is . . .

Instantaneous . . . pure, conscious awareness. Continuous Presence . . .

This 'I' had 'merged' into an 'Ocean of Nectar'. The ego-self had totally vanished.

It was not possible to speak after this event for many hours. Later, I painted a mandala which was full of light as were the brush, the paper and the paint. Light energy continued dancing around for a long time. No thoughts could touch it.

There was nothing to search for. Who was there to search for . . . what? This little spark of consciousness, this vibration of the vast universe had returned 'Home'. This was pure Illuminated Consciousness. I no longer saw myself as something separate from anything or anyone else. I knew that whatever I did or said, affected everyone and everything else around me because 'everyone and everything' was also 'me'. The focus had shifted from a personal 'me' to the all-encompassing reality.

'I' could now comprehend that the world was literally a manifestation from my own mind. If my mind was 'not there' then the world did not exist. No words could ever define such an experience.

Was this was the life-changing experience that the Glastonbury palmist had seen in my hand some four years before?

For a while, I was not conscious in the normal way but did whatever needed to be done, feeling no concern at all for the physical self. There was no attachment to what was being done. I fell and sprained my ankle whilst visiting a friend and my consciousness was jolted into a terrible darkness. Instantly, 'I' *experienced* the pain of separation—the sensation of 'separation' from that natural state of bliss. I surrendered everything to that luminosity within which is my true nature.

The darkness was gone as quickly as it had come.

A friend comes to visit me. The sun is shining through her hair, bathing it in sunlight. I just marvel at the beauty and intensity. Everything is so conscious and alive.

Everything has changed . . . yet nothing has changed.

This life is a petal that I offer to that core of my Being.

A fleeting moment that is Eternity.

This Consciousness,

Divine, Pure,

In the Dance of Reality.

Here and There,

Not out nor in.

Nor is or is not

I am Home.

. . .

satguru

"...Oh ocean of bliss embracing
My small being
A soothing balm to my consciousness
Precious jewel
A lotus for my feet
I walk at one with You
Never to leave my heart now
You have stolen me
From the world . . ."

(*Poems from My Heart*, 'This Hill')

35 ascent

SITTING OUTSIDE SKANDASRAMAM. The sun is
shining. The birds are singing.

The breeze rustles the leaves of the nearest tree . . .
I am called by my Father . . .

He says 'Come My Beloved. Come to Me.'

A companion appears . . . A delightful, shining soul
to lead the way.

We depart without a sound and steal away up the
beckoning tracks.

Every stone sings Your praises caressing my feet

as I walk lightly on You Arunachala—Mother-Father
of my heart.

Each stone is illuminated—a dazzling necklet of
gems on Your pure robe.

Many beings walk on Your surface. You love them all
and I

lightly walk barefoot with care so as not to injure
even one of Your devotees.

Oh beautiful Arunachala!

Whose brow is covered by dancing dragonflies

Whose Heart is full of painted butterflies

Whose raiment is the green of the trees

Whose perfume of the many-coloured flowers
intoxicates the Lover.

Whose feet are the red stones of fire

Whose aura is the blue sky

Whose sound is the wind in the leaves and grasses
chanting Om Om Om

Oh Heart You sing Your sweet lullaby

Of Peace and Love

Of Strength and Fortitude

Of Healing and Liberation

Oh Ramana

Who whispers words of Love in my Heart—the
Source

To the sounds of a flute wafting on Your sweet breath

You wrap Your cloak of indigo and star-spangled sky

SAT GURU

A crescent moon caressing Your brow

Your sweet embrace holds me close

And You sing

'Come My Beloved. Come to Me.'

final word

This has been a story

A true story some might say . . .

But in the 'In-lightened' moment

A story is a

Figment of the imagination

A fabrication of the mind

Through the loss of the 'I'

'I' am Eternal

There is no story

For who is there to tell it

And who is there to listen?

'Who Am I?'

Bhagavan Sri Ramana Maharshi

The pure Self is not realised unless the mind subsides.

The mind is nothing but a bundle of thoughts, and the first and foremost of all thoughts is the primal 'I' thought.

Therefore, only through the enquiry 'Who Am I?' does the mind subside.

To keep the mind constantly turned within and to abide thus in the Self is alone Self Enquiry.

By steady and continuous investigation into the nature of the mind, the mind is transformed into THAT to which the 'I' refers, and that is verily the Self.

That which arises in the physical body as 'I,' is the mind.

If one enquires whence this I-ness first arises, it will be found that it is the Heart or *Hridayam*.

Restraint of the out-going mind and its absorption in the Heart is known as *Antarmukha-drishti* or introversion.

When the mind becomes absorbed in the Heart the 'I' or ego vanishes, and the pure Consciousness or Self, which subsists during all the states of the mind, alone remains resplendent.

This state, where there is not the slightest trace of the 'I'-thought, is one's true *Swarupa*.

And that is called Quiescence or *Mouna*; that is also true Wisdom.

The Self alone exists; and the Self alone is real.

Verily the Self alone is the world, the 'I' and God.

All that exists is but the manifestation of the Supreme Being.

APPENDIX

Firm and disciplined inherence in the Self does verily constitute self-surrender to the Supreme Lord.

Let any amount of burden be laid on Him. He doth bear it all.

That which is Bliss is verily the Self. And THAT alone is real.

Not even in one of the countless objects of the world is there anything that can be called happiness.

This phenomenal world is nothing but thought.

When the mind is free from thought it enjoys the Bliss of the Self.

The mind of the Enlightened One never exists apart from the Self Absolute or *Brahman*.

Likes and dislikes, love and hatred, are equally to be eschewed.

It is not proper to let the mind rest often on the objects or affairs of mundane life.

If the ego subsides all else will also subside.

The deeper the humility with which we conduct ourselves, the better it is for us.

Everything that is offered to others is really an offering to oneself.

Not to desire anything extraneous to oneself is *Vairagya* or Dispassion.

Not to give up one's hold on the Self is *Jnana* or Enlightenment.

Thus *Vairagya* and *Jnana* are really one and the same.

Pledged to *Vairagya*, every aspirant must dive deep into himself and realize the precious *Atman*, the Self Absolute.

God and *Guru* are one.

He that has earned the Grace of *Guru* shall undoubtedly be saved and never be forsaken.

But the disciple, for his part, should follow the path shown by the Master.

Quotation from *Bhagavan Sri Ramana: A Pictorial Biography*. Published with the kind permission of Sri V. S. Ramanan, President, Sri Ramanasramam, Tiruvannamalai, South India.

recommended reading

Be As You Are: The Teachings of Sri Ramana Maharshi
Edited by David Godman, Penguin/Arkana, 1985

Advaita Bodha Deepika: The Lamp of Non-Dual Knowledge
Translated into English from the Sanskrit by
Sri Ramanananda Saraswathi (Munagala Venkataramiah)
Published by V.S. Ramanan, President, Sri Ramanasramam,
Tiruvannamalai—606603, India, 2002

The Heart of Awareness: A Translation of the Ashtavakra Gita
Translated by Thomas Byrom
Shambhala, Boston, 1990

The Song of Ribhu
English translation of the Tamil *Ribhu Gita*
by Dr. H. Ramamoorthy and Nome
Special Edition published by arrangement with
Society of Abidance in Truth, California, USA
by V.S. Ramanan, President, Sri Ramanasramam,
Tiruvannamalai—606603, India, 2003

You Are the Eyes of the World
by Longchenpa, translated by Kennard Lipman and Merrill Peterson,
Introduction by Namkhai Norbu Rinpoche,
Snow Lion Publications, Ithaca, NY, USA, 2000

The Crystal and the Way of Light:
Sutra, Tantra, and Dzogchen; The Teachings of Namkhai Norbu
Compiled and edited by John Shane
Routledge and Kegan Paul, London, 1986

The Tenth Man
by Wei Wu Wei
Hong Hong University Press

Choiceless Awareness
by J. Krishnamurti
Krishnamurti Publications of America
Ojai, California, USA, 1992

Nandini gives regular satsangs
in Glastonbury, London and
elsewhere under the auspices of the
Ramana Maharshi Foundation UK.

For further details please visit
www.advaitaspirit.org or e-mail
~~bishop@arunachala.fsworld.co.uk~~

nandinigrace@gmail.com